The 7 evil spirits

Shamah-Elim Bible Studies
http://shamah-elim.info

Shamah-Elim
שָׁמָּה אֵילִם

Noe Leon

All the Biblical passages quoted in this book are from the original King James Version, which is in the public domain; all emphases in Bible quotes were added by us.

Explanations of Hebrew, Aramaic, and Greek words are derived from information in the Enhanced Strong's Lexicon (©1995, Logos Research Systems, Inc.) included in software from Logos Research Systems, Inc. (www.logos.com). We generally use the Enhanced Strong's Lexicon and other word-meaning sources as references, deriving our own conclusions from the information they present and from other facts related to the original Hebrew, Greek, and Aramaic texts that we may find independently.

ISBN: 978-1-84799-644-2

Table of Contents

4

An overview

Our 7-faceted nature

According to Scripture, there are 7 Spirits of God (Revelation 3:1), which means that God's nature is comprised of 7 interrelated facets. Since we were made in God's image and likeness (Genesis 1:26), we can immediately infer that the spectrum of man's nature is comprised of the same 7 facets as God's nature. Thus, no human being can consider him or herself complete unless his or her 7 facets are fully developed. This is the reason why the Lord starts His Apocalypse message to the church in Sardis with the following words:

"¹And unto the angel of the church in Sardis write; These things saith he that hath the seven Spirits of God, and the seven stars; I know thy works, that thou hast a name that thou livest, and art dead. ²Be watchful, and strengthen the things which remain, that are ready to die: for I have not found thy works perfect before God." (Revelation 3:1-2, KJV)

Notice how the Lord introduces Himself as the One who has the 7 Spirits of God (v1) and then proceeds to indict the believers' works as "imperfect" (v2). The word "perfect" in verse 2 was mistranslated from the Greek verb *pleroo*, which literally means "to make full, to render full, to complete, to consummate". Therefore, God's reference to His 7 Spirits and to the believers' lack of "completion" or "fullness" is His way of saying,

> **"Your works shall be complete in My eyes if and only if you move in the fullness of My 7 Spirits"**

As you study Scripture in detail, it becomes evident that the spirit realm operates under a principle we could term "the parallel universe principle". It is as if everything in the realm of unrighteousness is a distorted reflection of something in the realm of righteousness. Therefore, it is not surprising that Scripture speaks of 7 types of evil spirits, which, upon further review, are actually corrupted forms of the 7 Spirits of God. These evil "anti-spirits" are represented in the 7 nations that the people of Israel had to fight against in order to conquer the Promised Land:

*"¹When the LORD thy God shall bring thee into the land whither thou goest to possess it, and hath cast out many nations before thee, the **Hittites**, and the **Girgashites**, and the **Amorites**, and*

the **Canaanites**, and the **Perizzites**, and the **Hivites**, and the **Jebusites**, seven nations greater and mightier than thou; *²And when the LORD thy God shall deliver them before thee; thou shalt smite them, and utterly destroy them; thou shalt make no covenant with them, nor shew mercy unto them" (Deuteronomy 7:1-2, KJV)*

To some, the nations listed above are nothing more than an "archaeological" footnote added by God to entertain believers interested in historical trivia. Such an attitude, however, that all the literal events experienced by the Israelites are shadows of events in the spirit realm:

"¹Now of the things which we have spoken this is the sum: We have such an high priest, who is set on the right hand of the throne of the Majesty in the heavens; ²A minister of the sanctuary, and of the true tabernacle, which the Lord pitched, and not man. ³For every high priest is ordained to offer gifts and sacrifices: wherefore it is of necessity that this man have somewhat also to offer. ⁴For if he were on earth, he should not be a priest, seeing that there are priests that offer gifts according to the law: ⁵Who serve unto the example and shadow of heavenly things, as Moses was admonished of God when he was about to make the tabernacle: for, See, saith he, that thou make all things according to the pattern shewed to thee in the mount." (Hebrews 8:1-5, KJV)

Thus, the seven nations listed in Deuteronomy 7:1, which were literal people in the past, now represent 7 "varieties" of evil spirits that each of us, and the Church as a whole, must overcome in order to enter into the Promised Land of God. This book is, in essence, a brief study of these 7 anti-spirits. It is important to understand the nature and *modus operandi* of each of these 7 anti-spirits because their presence hinders the development of the 7 Spirits of God in our lives and in the lives of others. God's purposes for mankind cannot be fulfilled unless these 7 evil spirits are nullified and annihilated.

Warfare

As you read this book, please bear in mind that these 7 evil spirits cannot be expelled from a person's life through a simple session of effusive prayer and an authoritative rebuke "in the name of Jesus". Neither will you find the people infected with these spirits foaming at the mouth and rotating their heads 360° (well, at least not most of them!). Even though these spirits do produce tangible consequences on the human body, their operations can only be seen as you discern the hearts of men, for these spirits are able to make a "home" of Earth by establishing invisible roots in the hearts of men and women. As you meditate on what God has to say about these evil spirits, you will begin to discern the **Girgashite** spirit, for example, in your neighbour Tom who has the nasty habit of following "procedure" for procedure's sake. You will see the **Canaanite** spirit in your friend who guides her life by the opinions of others due to her compulsive desire to please people. You will see the **Jebusite** spirit in your uncle Luke who loves to humiliate people when they make minor mistakes. You will see the **Hittite** spirit in your bohemian friend Alf who hates all rules and is constantly investing his time fighting for radical but misguided causes. You will see the **Amorite** spirit in your tall friend Don who loves to use people and is obsessed with conquering the adulation of others. You will see the **Perizzite** spirit in your shy friend Lorrie who suffers from low self-esteem and who has decided that she will never amount to much in life. You will see the **Hivite** spirit in your lazy friend Durham who loves the "easy" life and is constantly scheming to make some fast money so that he can spend it in vain pleasures.

As you can see, there is nothing "glamorous" about recognising these spirits or fighting against them, for the battle against them entails attacking deep-seated roots in the hearts of men. In short, when you fight against these spirits, you are fighting to **awaken** people from the slumber of these spirits so that they may want to be free from them. Along this fight, you will encounter men and women who act as recalcitrant strongholds of these spirits on Earth, and, as you do, you will suffer through excruciatingly painful trials and tribulations. Through this difficult warfare, your life will lead to the fall and destruction of some and to the liberation of others, all so that God's Kingdom may be established on Earth. Most of this warfare shall be silent and invisible, and it will be played out in the stage of your daily living. At the end, however, God will reveal to all the fruits of your work, and you will realise that it was all worthwhile, like a mother who forgets all her labour pains when she holds her newborn child in her arms.

Final introductory notes

As you read this book, please bear in mind that we may use any of the 7 spirit names to refer either to a **spirit** or to a **person**. If we refer to a "Girgashite", for example, we may be referring either to a Girgashite **spirit** or to a **person** "infected" with that type of spirit.

You may find articles and prophetic words related to the 7 evil spirits and other subjects on our Bible studies website: Shamah-Elim Bible Studies (http://shamah-elim.info).

Noe Leon
Shamah-Elim Bible Studies

Chapter 1
The Girgashites

This chapter will focus on the "Girgashites", the most common type of evil spirit, and the one whose manifestations are – shall we say – the least "spiritual".

An article similar to this chapter is posted on the Shamah-Elim Bible Studies website at the following web address:
http://shamah-elim.info/girgash.htm

What's in a name?

A great deal can be inferred directly from the meaning of the word "Girgashite". The name "Girgashite" literally means, "clay dweller", which refers to "dwelling on **earthliness**". Therefore, we can say that the "Girgashite" spirit is a spirit of earthliness that promotes a focus on earthly, **temporal** things; the Girgashite spirit creates people who are focused on the **natural**, producing a disdain for things that are "spiritual" and **eternal**, thereby denying the truth of the following passage:

"For we know that if our earthly house of this tabernacle were dissolved, we have a building of God, an house not made with hands, eternal in the heavens." (2 Corinthians 5:1)

Notice how the verse above is contrary to the spirit of earthliness. It recognises the **temporality** of our **earthly** tabernacle and sets its sights on things that are **eternal** in the heavens. The verse prior to 2 Corinthians 5:1 reveals an interesting trait of the Girgashite spirit of earthliness:

*"While we look not at the **things which are seen**, but at the things which are not seen: for the things which are seen are temporal; but the things which are not seen are eternal." (2 Corinthians 4:18)*

Girgashites (i.e.- people infected with this type of spirit) tend to focus on things that are **visible**. The Greek word translated as "seen" in the verse above is *blepo*, which means, "to discern mentally, to understand, to set the mind's thoughts on a thing, to consider". Girgashites are very **analytical** people who base their life's decisions on the pros and cons that their minds are able to perceive. For example, when they have to decide between two job opportunities, they consider factors such as salary, distance from home, promotion opportunities, dental plans, and work schedule. When a believer allows Girgashite spirits to take root in his or her heart, he or she rarely considers whether God wants him or her to take the job with the lower salary, longer working hours, and no life insurance. God always has a higher plan in mind. He might want you to take the less appealing job because He wants to use you in a mighty way to influence the lives of the people at that job. God might be visualising past external benefits and warning you that satan is trying to entice you to take the other job in an effort to lure you away from your calling in Christ; the job may look good at the beginning but will slowly envelop you and eat you up alive.

Whereas Girgashites base their lives on the natural and visible, non-Girgashite believers are not easily distracted by what their minds can see. Instead, they focus on what **God wants** for their lives. When choosing between two jobs, the non-Girgashite believer goes to God in prayer and asks Him, "Lord, which job do You want me to take? Which one is in Your will?". God may respond that He wants the believer to take the lower-salary job, take the higher-salary job, or neither! Non-Girgashite believers are focused on the things that can't be seen, i.e.- the things that can't be discerned with the natural mind. Because of this, they may at times make decisions that sound completely illogical and nonsensical to fellow believers and family members who are Girgashite in their hearts:

"*12Now we have received, not the spirit of the world, but the spirit which is of God; that we might know the things that are freely given to us of God. 13Which things also we speak, not in the words which man's wisdom teacheth, but which the Holy Ghost teacheth; comparing spiritual things with spiritual. 14But the natural man receiveth not the things of the Spirit of God: for they are foolishness unto him: neither can he know them, because they are spiritually discerned. 15But he that is spiritual judgeth all things, yet he himself is judged of no man. 16For who hath known the mind of the Lord, that he may instruct him? But we have the mind of Christ." (1 Corinthians 2:12-16)*

As the passage above shows, the non-Girgashite does not rely on human wisdom, preferring instead to depend on the voice of the Holy Spirit (v13). The natural man (i.e.- the Girgashite) cannot receive the things of the Spirit because they sound foolish to him (v14). God eventually stops talking to Girgashite believers because, every time He does, they simply brush off His words as nonsense and proceed to do their own will based on what their natural minds perceive. If you prefer to rely on the voice of the Spirit rather than on your natural mind, you will begin to act according to the mind of Christ (v16), and you will be able to perceive things that others do not. You will perceive real dangers where others don't see them. You will begin to see spiritual doors that others don't see. And, according to verse 15 above, no one will have authority to "judge" you. In other words, when you begin to operate in the Spirit, you stand above the jurisdiction of natural man's criticism, so don't worry about what your brothers and sisters at church may say about you. Don't worry about what your wife, kids, brothers, or sisters may say. You just do what God has called you to do. As long as you are **sure** in your spirit that you are doing God's will, simply obey Him and let the chips fall where they may.

How to avoid being a Girgashite in your decisions

So far, we have talked about how Girgashites live out their lives relying mostly on the perceptions of their natural mind, undermining the voice of the Spirit. God gives us some guidelines to ensure that we really **are** hearing the voice of God on a given matter:

"[13]Who is a wise man and endued with knowledge among you? let him shew out of a good conversation his works with meekness of wisdom. [14]But if ye have bitter envying and strife in your hearts, glory not, and lie not against the truth. [15]This wisdom descendeth not from above, but is earthly, sensual, devilish. [16]For where envying and strife is, there is confusion and every evil work. [17]But the wisdom that is from above is first pure, then peaceable, gentle, and easy to be intreated, full of mercy and good fruits, without partiality, and without hypocrisy. [18]And the fruit of righteousness is sown in peace of them that make peace." (James 3:13-18)

Based on the passage above, the guidelines are the following:

❑ **Meekness in wisdom (v13)**
A "meek" person is a person who is easily led by another, the same way a meek horse is easily led by anyone who rides it. Is your soul meek towards God? Do you have a predisposition to be led by the Spirit to wherever He may take you, without regard for personal sacrifice and suffering? Are you willing to obey the voice of God above the voice of man, even at the risk of being left alone? If you are, you are a meek person, and you

11

will be acting in the wisdom of God because the beginning of wisdom is the **"fear of God"** (Proverbs 9:10), and the "fear of God" is the constant concern in a person's heart to please God and to do what is pleasant to Him. By contrast, **"fear of man"** is the concern to do what pleases men, even if it does not please God. To have "fear of man" is to be afraid of what man thinks. To have "fear of God" is to be afraid of what **God** thinks.

❑ **Not focusing on what can be seen with the natural mind (v15)**
Are you "earthly" (v15)? Are you a Girgashite "clay dweller"? Are you focused on what you can perceive and analyse with your mind? If you are, you are not likely to hear the voice of God.

❑ **Not focusing on personal agendas of self-aggrandisement (v15, 14, and 16)**
Are you "devilish" (v15)? Are you willing to step on whomsoever you have to in order to get to the top? Are you constantly looking out for "number one"? Are your decisions based on what benefits you (and your family) instead of basing them on what will glorify God on Earth? If that is the case, you are not likely to hear from God.

❑ **Willingness to judge, without showing emotional partiality (v15, 17, 18)**
The word "sensual" in verse 15 was mistranslated from the Greek word *psychikos*, which comes from the word *psyche* meaning, **"soul"** (this is the word from which "psychology", "psychiatry", and "psychic" are derived). Therefore, the word "sensual" should really say **"soulish"**. Since the most predominant part of the soul is formed by the emotions[1], soulish decisions tend to be greatly influenced by soulish emotion. Some choose the congregation they will attend, for example, because their great friends go there, not because God is there. Some choose the person they will marry because that person makes them "feel so good", not because they have the Holy Spirit's witness. Soulish judgements tend to wilfully ignore warning signs that the Spirit gives out. God might be warning a young lady, for example, that her fiancée, who makes her "feel so good", is a man with no spiritual depth who will eventually destroy her calling as a prophet. God might be warning a young man not to attend the

---

[1] We share on the 3 components of the soul in an article titled "The three levels of pastoring" posted on the Shamah-Elim Bible Studies website (http://shamah-elim.info/3lvlpast.htm).

congregation his buddies and girlfriend go to because the doctrine there will actually serve as a hindrance to his spiritual growth as an apostle. Soulish judgements tend to ignore these silent whispers of the Spirit, choosing instead to let their emotions be stirred up by what their natural mind can see, and making decisions based on those emotions.

Verse 17 above says that the Spirit of God want us to be "without partiality", "without hypocrisy". The Greek word translated as "without partiality" is **adiakritos**, which is a combination of three Greek words:

* **a**, which means, "without",
* **dia**, which means, "between, amongst", and
* **kritos**, which means, "judgement".

The word adiakritos, therefore, literally means, "without judging between". This refers to the type of action that most people perform, for example, when they go to the supermarket to buy fresh fruits. They go through the box of fruits, feeling each fruit with their hands, smelling them, "judging between" one fruit and the other, and taking the ones that they judge to be the freshest and most delicious. This is OK when you are buying fruits, but not with the things of God. In other words, you cannot choose between the things that God has spoken to your heart, picking the things you like and ignoring the things you don't like. Many believers love to buy the "fruit" of mercy, for example; they love to believe that God is a merciful and loving God, the Shepherd who provides for all of our needs. But when it comes time to buying the "fruit" of judgement, they simply ignore it and pretend as if it is not there; they would rather ignore the fact that God is Consuming Fire, that He is a Righteous and Holy God who abhors iniquity and loves justice; that fruit causes them emotional indigestion, so they prefer to leave it in the spiritual "fruit box". If you only listen to God when He tells you things you like to hear, and constantly ignore Him when He tells you to do something you don't like, God will eventually stop talking to you, and the mighty calling for your life will be wasted away.

The word translated as "without hypocrisy" in verse 18 is the Greek word **anypokritos**, which comes from combining three Greek words:

* **a**, meaning "without",
* **hypo**, meaning "under", and
* **kritos**, meaning "judgement".

The word anypokritos, therefore, literally means "without under-judging". "Under-judging" (i.e.- "hypo-crisy") is, in essence, the "art" of lowering your standards of judgement in order to favour those whom your soul loves, thus establishing "double standards"; this is the real meaning of the word "hypocrisy" in the Bible. A "hypocritical" or "under-judging" teacher, for example, might set an easy exam for the students she likes and a difficult one for the one she dislikes. A "hypocritical" or "under-judging" young lady might hate people who smoke and drink, but make an exception for the new boy in class, who is a smoker and a heavy drinker, but who is "oh, so cute!". Hypocritical people are those who change their judgement standards in order not to drive away those whom their souls love. Many people are hypocritical with themselves; in other words, their soul loves itself so much that they judge themselves with a standard more lenient than the one they apply to others.

Verse 18 of James 3 above also says that the fruit of "righteousness" or "justice" is sown in peace of them that "make peace". A close study of Jeremiah 8:11 and other passages[2] reveals that the peace that God is after is the "peace of the hearts", a peace in which our wills are at peace with His (the heart is where the will resides). This means that the true "peacemakers" of the Bible are those whose works of justice and righteousness make the people around them adapt their wills to the will of God. The peacemaker is the one whose actions make others want to end their "war of wills" with God, surrendering their wills to His calling and purpose for their lives. Isn't it interesting that James did not say "fruit of mercy", or "fruit of affection"? It is only through a manifestation of God's justice and judgement that we can bring others to true repentance and surrender to God's will. As Isaiah 32 shows, judgement produces justice, and justice yields true peace; a place where iniquity is tolerated and where God's judgements are rejected will never have true peace:

"[14]Because the palaces shall be forsaken; the multitude of the city shall be left; the forts and towers shall be for dens for ever, a joy of wild asses, a pasture of flocks; [15]Until the spirit be poured upon us from on high, and the wilderness be a fruitful field, and the fruitful field be counted for a forest. [16]Then judgment shall dwell in the wilderness, and righteousness remain in the fruitful field. [17]And the work of

[2] We share on the "3 peaces" in an article titled 'What is a "false prophet"?' posted on the Shamah-Elim Bible Studies website (http://shamah-elim.info/flsproph.htm).

righteousness shall be peace; and the effect of righteousness quietness and assurance for ever." (Isaiah 32:14-17)

Therefore, our decisions and judgements should be based on a zeal for justice, without picking only what we like and without lowering our judgement standards so as to favour those whom we love. If our decisions are without "hypocrisy", the voice of God will become constant and strong in your life, and you will fulfil the purpose for which you were placed on Earth.

Learning to hear God's voice is a growth process, and it's a growth that no one can do for you. If you have willingly become dependent on others (such as the pastor at your congregation), and you always have to go to them to know what God wants to say to you, you will never enter into spiritual maturity and you will never be all that God wants you to be:

"¹²For when for the time ye ought to be teachers, ye have need that one teach you again which be the first principles of the oracles of God; and are become such as have need of milk, and not of strong meat. ¹³For every one that useth milk is unskilful in the word of righteousness: for he is a babe. ¹⁴But strong meat belongeth to them that are of full age, even those who by reason of use have their senses exercised to discern both good and evil." (Hebrews 5:12-14)

Notice how verse 13 talks about being skilful in the word of **righteousness**, i.e.- the word of **justice**. A lack of zeal for the justice of God is a sign of spiritual immaturity.

As you continue to seek His kingdom and His righteousness in your life, your soul will become more and more synchronised with God's will. There will be times when God will ask you to do things that *will in fact be pleasant to your soul*, but satan will come and tell you that what you are hearing is not from God because your soul agrees with it. In other words, what you hear from God may or may not be pleasant to your soul, but, as long as you maintain your predisposition to do His will and to abide in His word of justice and judgement, you will continue to hear God and stay in His plan.

Based on the following passage, we can say that there are three things that we must ask concerning God's will:

"⁴Now there are diversities of gifts, but the same Spirit. ⁵And there are differences of administrations, but the same Lord. ⁶And

there are diversities of operations, but it is the same God which worketh all in all." (1 Corinthians 12:4-6)

1. **How?**
   Verse 4 declares that the Spirit (the Holy Spirit) is in charge of the gifts. The gifts are the "tools" that enable us to perform God's will. Therefore, they provide the "how".

2. **What?**
   Verse 5 declares that the Lord (God the Son), is in charge of the "administrations". The word translated as "administrations" is the Greek word *diakonia* (from which we get "deacon" in English). A better translation for *diakonia* is "ministries"; our ministries determine what God wants us to do.

3. **When?**
   Verse 6 declares that God (God the Father), is in charge of the "operations". This means that it is the Father who determines *when* a planned operation will get under way:

   "And he said unto them, It is not for you to know the times or the seasons, which the Father hath put in his own power." (Acts 1:7)

When trying to do God's will, you must take these three questions into consideration. Sometimes, we may want to do the right thing (we have the "what"), but we are trying to do it the wrong way (we don't have the "how"). Sometimes we are trying to do something at the right time (we have the "when"), but we are trying to do the wrong thing (we don't have the "what"). Therefore, we must learn to hear the answer to **all three** questions. The Lord Jesus will tell you what to do, and He will impress it in your **mind**; the Holy Spirit will tell you **how** to do it, and He will impress it in your **emotions**; the Father will tell you **when** to do it, and He will impress it in your **heart**.

When in doubt about God's will, you can always resort to fervent prayer. **Cry out and plead** unto God that He reveal His will to you, and He will respond, but you must be willing to accept anything He tells you to do:

"Call unto me, and I will answer thee, and shew thee great and mighty things, which thou knowest not." (Jeremiah 33:3)

"⁵If any of you lack wisdom, let him ask of God, that giveth to all men liberally, and upbraideth not; and it shall be given him. ⁶But let him ask in faith, nothing wavering. For he that wavereth is like a wave of the sea driven with the wind and tossed." (James 1:5-6)

The word translated as "wavering" in verse 6 above is the word *diakrino*, which comes from *dia*, meaning "between", and *krino*, meaning "to judge". In other words, *diakrino* means "to judge between, to judge amongst", which, as we explained on page 13, refers to the act of accepting only what you want to hear from God and rejecting what you don't want to hear. You must always **discern** what you read and what you hear in order to **judge** whether or not it is from God, including every sermon you hear at church or anything you read (like this book, for example). James 1:6, however, refers to judging something that your innermost being **already** knows as coming from God.

There is an interesting show called "Joan of Arcadia" (once aired on the CBS network in America and on Living in the UK). If you have a chance to watch repeats of this programme, I recommend that you do. It is interesting to observe how the main character, a teenager called Joan Girardi, is constantly being asked by God to perform tasks that are contrary to her soul's desires and to her natural thinking, and how, after a temper tantrum, she generally gets herself to do what God told her to do, finding out, as always, that God was right. This programme is a perfect example of how a Christian should learn to submit his or her will to the voice of God, not relying on human reason, as Girgashites do, or on soulish judgement. (By the way, some conservative Christians might object to God speaking to Joan through human form, sometimes as a young man, sometimes as an older woman, sometimes as an older man, but, to the prophetic remnant, this makes complete sense. God wants to manifest Himself through us. God wants to manifest Himself in our flesh, in the same way that He manifested Himself through the Lord Jesus whilst He was here in the flesh).

The Girgashite pigs

Believe it or not, the New Testament does make a little-known reference to the Girgashites:

"And when he was come to the other side into the country of the Gergesenes, there met him two possessed with devils, coming

out of the tombs, exceeding fierce, so that no man might pass by that way." (Matthew 8:28)

Some Greek manuscripts say "Gadarenes" instead of "Gergesenes" in the verse above, whilst others say "Gerasenes". Even though the region referred to in this passage is "Gadara" (and it's referred to as such in Mark 5:1), I am convinced in my being that, when Matthew wrote this verse in the original manuscript, he wrote "Gergesenes", which refers to the "Girgashite" people of Deuteronomy 7:1. Matthew 8:28, therefore, refers to a territory dominated by Girgashite spirits.

"28And when he was come to the other side into the country of the Gergesenes, there met him two possessed with devils, coming out of the tombs, exceeding fierce, so that no man might pass by that way. 29And, behold, they cried out, saying, What have we to do with thee, Jesus, thou Son of God? art thou come hither to torment us before the time? 30And there was a good way off from them an herd of many swine feeding. 31So the devils besought him, saying, If thou cast us out, suffer us to go away into the herd of swine. 32And he said unto them, Go. And when they were come out, they went into the herd of swine: and, behold, the whole herd of swine ran violently down a steep place into the sea, and perished in the waters. 33And they that kept them fled, and went their ways into the city, and told every thing, and what was befallen to the possessed of the devils. 34And, behold, the whole city came out to meet Jesus: and when they saw him, they besought him that he would depart out of their coasts." (Matthew 8:28-34)

Notice that, in this territory, "pig herding" seemed to be an important local industry. As we all know, pigs love to roll around in the mud, so they are a perfect representation of the Girgashite spirit, since "Girgashite" means "clay dweller". Girgashites are constantly focused on earthly things, in the same way that pigs are always looking towards the ground to find something to eat. I have heard that it is physically impossible for pigs to look up at the sky (I have never asked a pig if this is true, but it sounds true to me); this makes sense since the Girgashite spirit leads people away from focusing on heavenly things, on things of eternal nature, on the things above.

When the spirits in the possessed men left their bodies, they went into the pigs, and the whole herd ran violently down a steep incline into the sea, drowning in the waters (v32). This happened as a prophetic figure of what happens to people who allow their hearts to be dominated by Girgashite spirits, as we will see in the next paragraphs.

Much like the pigs of Matthew 8:32, Girgashite people are "violent runners". Since they rarely take the time to ask God what He wants, they usually make impulsive decisions based on a short-sighted vision that is completely focused on the ground. Girgashites make decisions the way a bull charges towards the bullfighter's cape.

Just like the pigs of Matthew 8:32, Girgashites die by "drowning". Drowned animals were declared an abomination in Scripture (Genesis 9:4, Leviticus 17:10-16, Acts 15:19) because they died with the blood inside of them. Why is that an abomination to God? Because the life of the flesh is in the blood (Leviticus 17:11). In other words, the "blood" represents our soul life (our *psyche*, as it is called in Greek). This means that a drowned animal represents a person who died without shedding his or her blood, without pouring out his or her life for the sake of others. The Lord Jesus shed His blood; He poured out His soul existence so that we might have spiritual life, and God calls us all to do the same thing for the sake of others. Girgashites are **selfish** people. "Me", "myself", and "I" are the Girgashite's best friends, and he is interested in blessing no one but himself and his closest family members. Since Girgashites assign so much importance to **temporal** life, they are unwilling to shed it in sacrifice, because they don't believe that you can reap **eternity** when you sow in temporality. They might say with their lips that they believe in "eternal life", but, in their hearts, they really don't really live out that belief. When push comes to shove, they don't believe the following words:

"*[42]So also is the resurrection of the dead. It is sown in corruption; it is raised in incorruption: [43]It is sown in dishonour; it is raised in glory: it is sown in weakness; it is raised in power: [44]It is sown a natural body; it is raised a spiritual body. There is a natural body, and there is a spiritual body. [45]And so it is written, The first man Adam was made a living soul; the last Adam was made a quickening spirit. [46]Howbeit that was not first which is spiritual, but that which is natural; and afterward that which is spiritual. [47]The **first man is of the earth, earthy**: the **second man is the Lord from heaven**. [48]As is the earthy, such are they also that are earthy: and as is the heavenly, such are they also that are heavenly. [49]And as we have borne the image of the earthy, we shall also bear the image of the heavenly. [50]Now this I say, brethren, that flesh and blood cannot inherit the*

19

kingdom of God; neither doth corruption inherit incorruption." (1 Corinthians 15:42-50)

[Notice how Paul uses the word "earthy" in verses 47-49, making an implicit reference to the Girgashite spirit]

When you meet the Lord on that fateful day, will He find you with blood inside of you, or will He see that you shed your blood as a living sacrifice so that others might have life? If He finds blood in you, you will be an abomination to Him, and He will cast you away from Him. He abhors selfishness, so He cannot make Himself One with a person who lived in self-centredness. His nature is one of selflessness, so He cannot be One with a person who is not selfless. God wants you to dwell in Him for eternity. **God Himself** wants to be your tabernacle, your house for eternity:

"¹For we know that if our earthly house of this tabernacle were dissolved, we have a building of God, an house not made with hands, eternal in the heavens. ²For in this we groan, earnestly desiring to be clothed upon with our house which is from heaven: ³If so be that being clothed we shall not be found naked. ⁴For we that are in this tabernacle do groan, being burdened: not for that we would be unclothed, but clothed upon, that mortality might be swallowed up of life. ⁵Now he that hath wrought us for the selfsame thing is God, who also hath given unto us the earnest of the Spirit. ⁶Therefore we are always confident, knowing that, whilst we are at home in the body, we are absent from the Lord: ⁷(For we walk by faith, not by sight:) ⁸We are confident, I say, and willing rather to be absent from the body, and to be present with the Lord. ⁹Wherefore we labour, that, whether present or absent, we may be accepted of him. ¹⁰For we must all appear before the judgment seat of Christ; that every one may receive the things done in his body, according to that he hath done, whether it be good or bad. ¹¹Knowing therefore the terror of the Lord, we persuade men; but we are made manifest unto God; and I trust also are made manifest in your consciences." (2 Corinthians 5:1-11)

[Notice how verse 7 refers to walking by faith, not by **sight**. Girgashites are sight-oriented walkers. They act solely on what their natural minds perceive.]

"²²And I saw no temple therein: for the Lord God Almighty and the Lamb are the temple of it. ²³And the city had no need of the sun, neither of the moon, to shine in it: for the glory of God did lighten it, and the Lamb is the light thereof. ²⁴And the nations of them which are saved shall walk in the light of it: and the kings of the earth do bring their glory and honour into it. ²⁵And the

gates of it shall not be shut at all by day: for there shall be no night there. ²⁶And they shall bring the glory and honour of the nations into it. ²⁷And there shall in no wise enter into it any thing that defileth, neither whatsoever worketh abomination, or maketh a lie: but they which are written in the Lamb's book of life." (Revelation 21:22-27)

Contrary to popular belief, the "Lamb's book of life" referred to in verse 27 above is not the list of those who were saved from going to hell. Instead, it is the book of those who will be made One with God for eternity because they were willing to sow what was temporary to reap what is eternal. There are many believers who will not be made One with Him. Many will live outside the New Jerusalem and regret having lived a life that proved to be an abomination to God. Notice how verse 27 clearly declares that nothing that "works abomination" will enter the New Jerusalem, and as we mentioned above, God will consider a believer to be an "abomination" if he or she dies with his or her blood inside on account of having lived a selfish life that was never willing to shed itself in loving sacrifice for the sake of God's plans in the lives of others.

Grunting versus groaning

As 2 Corinthians 5:2-4 (quoted above) shows, we are called to "groan" in order to be clothed in God's eternity. "Groaning" is produced by a soul that deeply desires and yearns for something without which it feels incomplete. This means that our souls should feel **incomplete** in our temporality, deeply longing and fervently striving towards being enveloped in God's eternity. Groaners have set their hopes on a higher vision, on a higher calling.

As we saw in the previous section, people dominated by Girgashite spirits are like pigs violently running down a steep incline, on their way to drowning in the sea. Girgashites are not groaners. They have relinquished living for a higher vision, deciding in their hearts that they can be **complete** in their temporality. This turns them into greedy pigs that grunt all day, devouring everything in sight in order to prove to themselves that temporary things can really make them complete. But, since it is **completely impossible** for a human being to find completeness in temporary things, the Girgashite's devouring becomes an ever increasing hunger that will **never** be satisfied. In Numbers 11, a people possessed by Girgashite spirits demanded flesh from God:

"⁴And the mixt multitude that was among them fell a lusting: and the children of Israel also wept again, and said, Who shall give us flesh to eat? ⁵We remember the fish, which we did eat in Egypt freely; the cucumbers, and the melons, and the leeks, and the onions, and the garlick: ⁶But now our soul is dried away: there is nothing at all, beside this manna, before our eyes." (Numbers 11:4-6)

Notice how the children of Israel allowed themselves to be led by their natural perceptions of the food they used to eat in Egypt. Their cry for "flesh" is a figure of a hunger for earthly things, since our flesh represents the clay from which we were made. Thus, the children of Israel were gripped by a Girgashite "clay-dwelling" spirit. Since Girgashites disdain the things from above (the things of the Spirit), the children of Israel showed utter disdain for the manna that fell from heaven. Therefore, they chose to "grunt" for flesh, and, towards the end of Numbers 11, God sends them the flesh they so strongly grunted for, but look at the consequences:

"³¹And there went forth a wind from the LORD, and brought quails from the sea, and let them fall by the camp, as it were a day's journey on this side, and as it were a day's journey on the other side, round about the camp, and as it were two cubits high upon the face of the earth. ³²And the people stood up all that day, and all that night, and all the next day, and they gathered the quails: he that gathered least gathered ten homers: and they spread them all abroad for themselves round about the camp. ³³And while the flesh was yet between their teeth, ere it was chewed, the wrath of the LORD was kindled against the people, and the LORD smote the people with a very great plague. ³⁴And he called the name of that place Kibrothhattaavah: because there they buried the people that lusted." (Numbers 11:31-34)

The word "Kibrothhattaavah" in verse 34 means "graves of desire" or "graves of covetousness". The people went after the quails with the same greed that a hungry pig goes after food on the ground. Notice how hard they worked to gather the quails. They worked all that day, all that **night**, and all the next day (v32). Because of their focus on earthliness, Girgashites are generally **sleep-deprived workaholics** who never seem to be able to relax. Insomnia is a condition of the mind provoked by the presence of Girgashite spirits in a person's heart. Girgashites diligently work to find completeness in their temporary endeavours, envisioning the day when they will have saved enough money to retire, move to Hawaii or the Canary Islands, and play golf all day. Unfortunately for them, Girgashites generally never get to enjoy the possessions they work so long and hard for. Just like the children of Israel in Numbers 11:33, they seem to die just before they start chewing their hard-earned quails:

"*13And one of the company said unto him, Master, speak to my brother, that he divide the inheritance with me. 14And he said unto him, Man, who made me a judge or a divider over you? 15And he said unto them, Take heed, and beware of covetousness: for a man's life consisteth not in the abundance of the things which he possesseth. 16And he spake a parable unto them, saying, The ground of a certain rich man brought forth plentifully: 17And he thought within himself, saying, What shall I do, because I have no room where to bestow my fruits? 18And he said, This will I do: I will pull down my barns, and build greater; and there will I bestow all my fruits and my goods. 19And I will say to my soul, Soul, thou hast much goods laid up for many years; take thine ease, eat, drink, and be merry. 20But God said unto him, Thou fool, this night thy soul shall be required of thee: then whose shall those things be, which thou hast provided? 21So is he that layeth up treasure for himself, and is not rich toward God.*" (Luke 12:13-21)*

It is interesting to note that the passage above starts with a person concerned about receiving a temporary inheritance. For the Girgashite, this world **is** his inheritance. Even though Girgashite believers may say that they believe in an eternal inheritance[3], they live as if that inheritance did not exist. Instead of groaning for the eternal prize, they keep grunting for more and more temporary possessions.

Why would someone prefer to grunt?

The answer to this question can be found in the verses prior to some passages we have already quoted in this chapter:

"*16For which cause we faint not; but though our outward man perish, yet the inward man is renewed day by day. 17For our light affliction, which is but for a moment, worketh for us a far more exceeding and eternal weight of glory; 18While we look not at the things which are seen, but at the things which are not seen: for the things which are seen are temporal; but the things which are not seen are eternal.*" (2 Corinthians 4:16-18)*

---

[3] There is an article posted on the Shamah-Elim Bible Studies website titled "What is your inheritance?" that shares on the eternal inheritance that God has for us (http://shamah-elim.info/inherit.htm).

The Girgashite prefers to anchor his or her vision to the ground because he or she understands that raising his or her vision implies the willingness to pay a price. This is why verse 17 speaks of a light and **temporary** affliction that is insignificant in comparison to the "**eternal** weight of glory" that we will reap if we are only willing to make the temporary sacrifice. Living for a higher vision, living for a higher calling, implies making sacrifices which become avoidable if we just lower our vision to the ground and pretend as if the higher calling does not exist. Imagine all the trouble that Martin Luther the Reformer would have saved himself if he had just been willing to work within the system and pretend that everything was OK. He was a respected monk with a nice teaching position at the University of Wittenberg. Why did he have to nail those 95 theses on that church door on October 31, 1517, and start the Protestant Reformation? He would have saved himself from much condemnation and isolation if he had just kept his mouth shut. Imagine all the trouble Martin Luther King Jr. would have saved himself if he had resigned himself to being a "nice" Southern American pastor of a small congregation. He would have lived a nice quiet life, and he might even be alive today! But, instead, he decided to stand up for what he believed; he decided to follow God's calling for his life; he decided to suffer imprisonment, physical aggression, and even assassination in order to pursue God's calling for his life. To this day, the lives of these men are still blessing countless numbers of people because they were not willing to live as selfish pigs, choosing instead to shed their lives as living sacrifices so that God's purposes could be fulfilled in the lives of others.

So much more to say

There is a great deal more to say about the Girgashites. For example, the Girgashite spirit is strongly related to diseases such as cancer and ADD (Attention Deficit Disorder). It is ironic that a spirit that focuses people on the visible is the invisible source of so many problems on Earth.

"*[1]If ye then be risen with Christ, seek those things which are above, where Christ sitteth on the right hand of God. [2]Set your affection on things above, not on things on the earth. [3]For ye are dead, and your life is hid with Christ in God. [4]When Christ, who is our life, shall appear, then shall ye also appear with him in glory. [5]Mortify therefore your members which are upon the earth; fornication, uncleanness, inordinate affection, evil concupiscence, and covetousness, which is idolatry*" (Colossians 3:1-5)

"[8]For my thoughts are not your thoughts, neither are your ways my ways, saith the LORD. [9]For as the heavens are higher than the earth, so are my ways higher than your ways, and my thoughts than your thoughts." (Isaiah 55:8-9)

To learn more about the Girgashite spirit, we recommend the following postings from the Shamah-Elim Bible Studies website:

- Article "The stingy enemies of God" (http://shamah-elim.info/stgenemy.htm)
- Prophetic word "Hurricane Frances" (http://shamah-elim.info/p_hurrfran.htm)
- Article "Bread sowing" (http://shamah-elim.info/breadsow.htm)
- Prophetic word "Wheat among corn" (http://shamah-elim.info/p_wheatcrn.htm)
- Article "Pre-parousia – Internal turmoil" (http://shamah-elim.info/preparu2.htm)
- Prophetic word "Flooded land" (http://shamah-elim.info/p_flood.htm)
- Prophetic word "The sun is burning out" (http://shamah-elim.info/p_sunburnt.htm)
- Prophetic word "The Kennedy curse" (http://shamah-elim.info/p_kennedy.htm)
- Prophetic word "Flight 358" (http://shamah-elim.info/p_flite358.htm)

Chapter 2
The Jebusites

This chapter will focus on the "Jebusites", a very "close relative" of the Girgashites. There are many similarities between the two. However, as we shall see, the Jebusites are more "militant" in their behaviour and a tad more focused on "invisible" things; yet, they end up being as "naturally minded" as the Girgashites, unable to recognise the true and deep things of the Spirit.

An article similar to this chapter is posted on the Shamah-Elim Bible Studies website at the following web address:
http://shamah-elim.info/jebusite.htm

What's in a name?

A great deal can be inferred directly from the meaning of the word "Jebusite". The name "Jebusite" literally means "thresher", which refers to the agricultural activity of beating grain out of the husk. This was usually done through animals such as oxen, which were used to tread on the grain that was laid out over a "threshing-floor". From this, we can infer that Jebusite spirits, being "threshers", are spirits that tread or "stomp" on other people. People whose hearts are "infected" by Jebusite spirits tend to be people who do not hesitate to put down and humiliate others. By stomping on people, Jebusites make a concerted effort to prevent them growing taller. They like to make people feel small, and they deliberately put "small" people down any time they see these "small" people asserting their authority. Jebusites believe that certain people are inherently inferior, without a right to manifest any kind of authority. According to Jebusites, "small" people should just shut up and concede because they are "nobodies" who will never amount to much. As some of you might already be thinking, the spirit of racism is a Jebusite spirit. Jebusites are **enforcers of social castes**.

Unfortunately, the Church is currently swarmed by Jebusites. In the past, these Jebusites took the form of legalistic believers who preached a "gospel" of Pharisaic rules and regulations. Under this "gospel", believers were taught to abide by and obey religious regulations without being told of their potential in Christ. Passages in Isaiah chapters 7 through 10 indicate that God had prophesied thousands of years ago that this legalistic spirit (represented by Rezin the king of Syria and Pekah the son of Remaliah, king of Israel) would be defeated and be replaced by a gospel more focused on our grace in Christ (represented by the king of Assyria). Isaiah chapters 9 and 10 show, however, that the "king of Assyria" would outstay his welcome, and that this "grace-aware" gospel would degenerate into a "gospel" without justice and judgement, a "gospel" in which iniquity was tolerated, a "gospel" in which mercy without truth would be the normal practice. Since this grace-aware gospel deviated from God's nature, it acted like an antibiotic that partially kills a virus but leaves enough of it so that it can mutate and become a strain of the virus more resistant to antibiotics than before. This is precisely what happened to the Jebusite spirit.

The Jebusite spirit is still swarming the Church, like a bad fly infestation, but not in its previous "legalistic" strain. It now takes on a subtler, less conspicuous form. The Jebusite spirit now preaches a "gospel" where the Body of Christ is divided into two main castes, **"ministers"**, and **"laymen"**. The "ministers" are the full-time pastors and their "church staff". The "laymen" are the "regular" church-going folks who do not hold a major position in the church "hierarchy". The so-called "ministers" become the spiritual gurus of the Church, and they are there to assist the less spiritually-inclined "laymen" who don't have the time or capability to hear directly from God, and, who, therefore, are spiritually ignorant in comparison to the "ministers". A relationship of dependency is thereby established between these two spiritual castes, a relationship in which the laymen surrender their spiritual authority to the ministers. Since the ministers are the only ones who can be relied on to really hear from God, everything the pastor says or does becomes the law of the land, and any layman who dares to question the teachings or the orders of the pastor (or any of his ordained staff) is automatically reprimanded and stomped on. "How dare anyone question the spiritual wisdom of the pastor?", the Jebusites say, adding,

> "Haven't you read Romans chapter 13? You are **supposed to** submit to authority; just obey, and you will be showered with the spiritual blessings provided by the authorities established by God. Rebel, and the covering of spiritual blessings will be taken away from you, and you will suffer the dire consequences of your disobedience."

Since this is a more "lenient" strain of the Jebusite virus than the one in the past, today's "ministers" give their "laymen" more freedoms. Young people can listen to satanic-style Heavy Metal music, as long as the lyrics are remotely "Christian". Young ladies can wear those provocative jeans and those tight tops that are so "in vogue", as long as their private parts are not "exposed", and as long as they continue to attend youth services. Choir singers can spend their entire life obsessed with their business dealings, without spending time to hear God's voice in their hearts, as long as they show up for all the choir practices and play their musical notes correctly. Deacons can spread nasty rumours about other brothers and sisters, as long as they have perfect attendance in all of their deacon activities. The co-pastor and his family can watch television programs with explicit messages promoting fornication and adultery, as long as they do not watch full-blown pornography, and as long as the pastor fulfils all of his co-pastoral responsibilities at church. All of this is allowed, but **watch out** if anyone dares to question the pastor's vision. That would be a sin!!! *"Just submit yourself and receive your blessings from your minister"*, is the battle cry of the modern-day Jebusite.

Submission unto eternal life

Please don't misunderstand me. From the section above, some might conclude that I do not believe in submission, but I **do** believe in having a submissive spirit. The Word calls us to submit **our entire being** to God. If God tells you to do a back flip, you must do it. If God calls you to stand on your head and drink a glass of water, you must do it. We must be willing to do **anything** God tells us to do. We are to present a submissive and meek heart before God. We are to be like clay that God can mould into **anything** He wants. In our submission to Him, we will also submit to man when we discern the voice of God speaking through that man (or woman):

"[27]My sheep hear my voice, and I know them, and they follow me: [28]And I give unto them eternal life; and they shall never perish, neither shall any man pluck them out of my hand. [29]My Father, which gave them me, is greater than all; and no man is able to pluck them out of my Father's hand. [30]I and my Father are one." (John 10:27-30)

As His sheep, we all have the capability to discern His voice and to know when **God** is speaking through man, as opposed to when *natural man* is speaking "in the name of God". As His sheep, we all have access to **eternal life** (v28), which is more than just escaping from literal hell[4]. A close study of passages such as Isaiah 33:14-17, Romans 2:7, 1 Timothy 6:12, Revelation 3:5, and Revelation 22:19

---

[4] We share more on this in an article titled "Are you a wide-gate believer?" posted on the Shamah-Elim Bible Studies website (http://shamah-elim.info/widegate.htm), under the section "Hezekiah's eternal loss".

reveals that "eternal life" is not "automatically granted" when you are born again; instead, it is the prize that has been made accessible to us if we persevere until the end (our perseverance is through surrender, not through human effort). The prize if we persevere is **to be made One with God for eternity**. That is eternal life, and not all who escape from the torments of literal hell shall experience it, just as not all the Israelites who left Egypt reached the Promised Land. Some believers shall be shunned by the Lord on that final day. They will not be sent to literal hell, but they shall not be allowed to approach God for all of eternity, and will forever be tagged as "those who chose to be eternally incompatible with God".

The fact that "eternal life" means "being made One with God for eternity" is the reason why the Lord ends the passage above (v30) with the statement, "I and My Father are One". Some might argue that only Jesus had the right to say this, but notice what Jesus says after verse 30:

"*[31]Then the Jews took up stones again to stone him. [32]Jesus answered them, Many good works have I shewed you from my Father; for which of those works do ye stone me? [33]The Jews answered him, saying, For a good work we stone thee not; but for blasphemy; and because that thou, being a man, makest thyself God. [34]Jesus answered them, Is it not written in your law, I said, Ye are gods? [35]If he called them gods, unto whom the word of God came, and the scripture cannot be broken;"* (John 10:31-35)

Here, the Lord calls you, fellow believer, "**a god**". Some might insist here that the word "god" must be written with a lowercase "g", but, please remember that the original text of all the New Testament books was written entirely in lowercase Greek letters, so any discussion over the "g" being a lowercase or an uppercase "g" is completely pointless. Such senseless discussions are derived from the fact that most believers are not aware of the **tremendous** implications of calling yourself a "*son of God*" or a "*daughter of God*". A dog's "descendants" are all dogs. A cat's "descendants" are all cats. A horse's "descendants" are all horses. So what can you expect God's descendants to be? If the answer to this question is much too troubling to us, we should stop calling ourselves "sons of God"!! In John 17, the Lord adds the following:

"*[21]That they all may be one; as thou, Father, art in me, and I in thee, that they also may be one in us: that the world may* *believe that thou hast sent me. ²²And the glory which thou gavest me I have given them; that they may be one, even as we are one" (John 17:21-22)*

Notice how Jesus is now saying that **we** have the opportunity to be One with the Father, just as He is One with Him. And notice how Jesus even dares to say that we may share in God's Glory!!! But notice what the Lord said through Isaiah:

"⁸I am the LORD: that is my name: and my glory will I not give to another, neither my praise to graven images." (Isaiah 42:8)

Is this a contradiction of what the Lord said in John 17:22? Since God does not share His Glory with anyone, no one can share in God's Glory **outside** of Him. This implies that the only way for Isaiah 42:8 and John 17:22 to be true at the same time is if we have an opportunity to be made One with God. This is the essence of eternal life, and this is why John 17 begins with the following passage:

"¹These words spake Jesus, and lifted up his eyes to heaven, and said, Father, the hour is come; glorify thy Son, that thy Son also may glorify thee: ²As thou hast given him power over all flesh, that he should give eternal life to as many as thou hast given him. ³And this is life eternal, that they might know thee the only true God, and Jesus Christ, whom thou hast sent." (John 17:1-3)

Eternal life, according to verse 3, is to **know** the "**One true**" God, which means, to know Him in His **Truth** and His **Oneness** (Deut 6:4). To be made One with the "**true**" God means becoming One with Him in **justice and judgement** because **truth** is intimately connected to justice and judgement[5], as certified by multiple passages throughout Scripture such as Psalm 15:1-2, 1 Kings 3:6, Psalm 96:13, Jeremiah 4:2, and Romans 2:2. You cannot become One with God unless you share and operate in God's judgements. If you abhor His judgement nature, you can never be made One with Him, for abhorring His judgement nature is equivalent to denying the God of truth, i.e.- the One **true** God.

Knowing that God is "One" implies believing that God will speak to you and breathe His judgement system and nature into you. How can a believer ever come to know God and be made One with Him if he or she is constantly being told that the only one who can

---

[5] We share more on this in an article titled "The spiritual Trojan horse" posted on the Shamah-Elim Bible Studies website (http://shamah-elim.info/trojnhrs.htm).

hear the voice of God is the pastor? Can you say that you know someone if you cannot recognise his voice? Can you really know someone who never talks to you? Can you really know someone who chooses to speak to you only through intermediaries who are "worthier" than you?

Jebusites do not understand that all believers have access to eternal life. Jebusites are very good at placing restrictions. They are good at limiting the lives of others, at telling them what they **can't** do, but they are **very bad** at teaching people about their potential, about all that they **can** be and do. Today's Jebusites have granted the "common" believer many freedoms in the **secular** arena, but continue to reserve **spiritual** freedom and potential for a selected few, thus denying God's "Oneness". Jebusites separate the One Body of Christ into two basic segments, the "ministerial" segment that can hear the voice of God, and the "layman" segment that is supposed to "submit to spiritual authority" and simply receive the blessings sent down to it by the more privileged "ministerial segment". If Jebusites truly believed in God's Oneness, they would have to admit that the Body of Christ is One and that God wants to permeate us with His Oneness so that He may become all in all (Psalm 133, 1 Corinthians 12:6, 1 Corinthians 15:28, Ephesians 1:23).

Jebusites do not understand that God operates by "death and resurrection". He first **kills** all that is contrary to Him through His Word of Judgement, which acts as a sword that comes to destroy all that is opposed to His nature in us (Hebrews 4:12), and then He **resurrects** us to a new nature in Him. This process of "death and resurrection" operates in us throughout our entire life on Earth. Jebusites understand the "death" part **very well**, but haven't quite grasped the "resurrection" part because they consider "small" believers to be unworthy of that resurrection life:

"*12Now if Christ be preached that he rose from the dead, how say some among you that there is no resurrection of the dead? 13But if there be no resurrection of the dead, then is Christ not risen: 14And if Christ be not risen, then is our preaching vain, and your faith is also vain. 15Yea, and we are found false witnesses of God; because we have testified of God that he raised up Christ: whom he raised not up, if so be that the dead rise not. 16For if the dead rise not, then is not Christ raised: 17And if Christ be not raised, your faith is vain; ye are yet in your sins. 18Then they also which are fallen asleep in Christ are perished. 19If in this life only we have hope in Christ, we are of all men most miserable." (1 Corinthians 15:12-19)*

"Resurrection life" is more than just being "alive" in Heaven after physical death. Fullness of resurrection life is to be made One with God, the Source and Author of Life Himself. If the word "resurrection" in Scripture simply means "coming back to life after physical death", why would Paul say that he wanted to somehow "attain His resurrection" (Philippians 3:11)? In the true and deep sense of the word, "resurrection" means "eternal life", and, as we said above, not all born-again believers shall attain eternal life (i.e.- eternal Oneness with God), even if they escape from the torment of literal hell.

Contrary to the Jebusite's belief, the condition for "growth-potential" in the Spirit is not a full-time pastoral ministry certified by some recognisable "spiritual" organisation, but rather a **heart submissive to God's will**, a heart that desires to live under God's constant judgements:

"*16And, behold, one came and said unto him, Good Master, what good thing shall I do, that I may have eternal life? 17And he said unto him, Why callest thou me good? there is none good but one, that is, God: but if thou wilt enter into life, keep the commandments. 18He saith unto him, Which? Jesus said, Thou shalt do no murder, Thou shalt not commit adultery, Thou shalt not steal, Thou shalt not bear false witness, 19Honour thy father and thy mother: and, Thou shalt love thy neighbour as thyself. 20The young man saith unto him, All these things have I kept from my youth up: what lack I yet? 21Jesus said unto him, If thou wilt be perfect, go and sell that thou hast, and give to the poor, and thou shalt have treasure in heaven: and come and follow me. 22But when the young man heard that saying, he went away sorrowful: for he had great possessions." (Matthew 19:16-22)*

When the young man asked Jesus how he could enter into "eternal life", Jesus did not ask him to repeat the sinner's prayer. He told him to keep the commandments. Jesus then proceeded to list 6 commandments. When the young man replied that he had kept all 6, Jesus did not say, "Liar, you do not keep them". Instead, He gave him a final commandment, commandment number **7**, which was to sell everything he had, give to the poor, and **follow** Him. The number "6" in Scripture generally represents human effort, since man is to work 6 days and rest on the 7th day (in a spiritual sense, of course). This means that, in order to enter into eternal life, there is an element of human effort involved, but the task can only be completed by

God. There is a part of the process where we must rest and allow **God** to work, and this is done by yielding to God. When Jesus asked the young man to sell his possessions, He was asking him to yield what was most precious to his heart. In other words, we can only enter eternal life through a **submissive** heart that yields **all** to God and is willing to **follow** Him wherever He takes us. We are called to **die** on the 7th day, so that we may **resurrect** on the **8th** day, just as Jesus was resurrected on the first day of the week following His death (Matthew 28:1-10).

Notice that Jesus did not tell the young man that the key element to eternal life was to submit to the priest at his local synagogue. The key to eternal life is to follow **Jesus**, not natural man. And, since we are supposed to know the voice of Jesus (John 10:27), we should be able to know when the pastor (or any human being on Earth) is speaking in the Spirit or not. When a pastor, or the young lad that sits next to you at church, is telling you something in the Spirit, you should obey, because it is God speaking. If the pastor speaks something that is contradictory to what God has revealed to your heart, you should **not** obey, because we are called to fear God more than man.

Jebusite-provoked lameness

In Acts chapter 3, Peter and John healed a lame man at the temple who begged by the gate called "The Beautiful":

"*¹Now Peter and John went up together into the temple at the hour of prayer, being the ninth hour. ²And a certain man lame from his mother's womb was carried, whom they laid daily at the gate of the temple which is called Beautiful, to ask alms of them that entered into the temple; ³Who seeing Peter and John about to go into the temple asked an alms. ⁴And Peter, fastening his eyes upon him with John, said, Look on us. ⁵And he gave heed unto them, expecting to receive something of them. ⁶Then Peter said, Silver and gold have I none; but such as I have give I thee: In the name of Jesus Christ of Nazareth rise up and walk. ⁷And he took him by the right hand, and lifted him up: and immediately his feet and ankle bones received strength. ⁸And he leaping up stood, and walked, and entered with them into the temple, walking, and leaping, and praising God. ⁹And all the people saw him walking and praising God: ¹⁰And they knew that it was he which sat for alms at **the Beautiful gate of the temple**: and they were filled with wonder and amazement at that which had happened unto him. ¹¹And as the lame man which* *was healed held Peter and John, all the people ran together unto them in the porch that is called Solomon's, greatly wondering." (Acts 3:1-11)*

The Spirit of God took the time to mention the fact that the gate's name was "the Beautiful" (v10). There is a spiritual reason for this. The concept of beauty is very much related to "grace". Therefore, this lame man represents all believers who have been left lame by the Jebusites and who don't realise that they are **so close** to the "gate of grace". Many believers are spiritually incapacitated, begging for the mercy of some "minister" who will come and give them some "alms" of spiritual blessing, without understanding that they themselves can have access to God's grace and a **direct** relationship with God. This grace does not mean having access to God in order to **simply get** things from God, as some believers think. This grace is in order **to know God** as a Father and as a Friend, to be One with Him, and to manifest His power and Glory on Earth (wouldn't you hate it if your children only approached you when they were interested in getting something from you?). This grace is to share in God's divine nature (2 Peter 1:3-4) and to manifest that nature on Earth. That is worth more than all the silver and gold in the world (v6).

Right before Peter and John healed the lame man in the name of Jesus, verse 7 declares that Peter took him by the right hand and **lifted** him. Notice how this is the opposite of what a Jebusite does, since Jebusites are bent on putting people down, not on lifting them up. Notice also that this lift went beyond an "emotional" lift. Christians are not supposed to be powerless "cheerleaders". The word "Christian" comes from the Greek word meaning "anointed", so Christians should be men and women that impart to people a **prophetic anointing** that projects them to the prophetic calling God has for them. That anointing is to be a **real** thing, a real substance in the spirit world. It is not emotional positivism. It is not soulish fluff.

After the lame man was healed, he walked, and entered with them into the temple (v8). This means that a true **apostolic** and **prophetic** anointing (represented by **Peter** and **John** respectively) enables fellow believers to walk on their own, ending their dependency on others. The lame man was now free to enter the temple and praise God on his own (v8). He entered into a direct relationship with God, the type of relationship that Jebusites strongly oppose. This is why the Spirit records the following passage in the chapter that follows the healing of the lame man:

*"¹And as they spake unto the people, the priests, and the captain of the temple, and the Sadducees, came upon them, ²**Being grieved that they taught the people**, and preached through Jesus the resurrection from the dead. ³And they laid hands on them, and put them in hold unto the next day: for it was now eventide. ⁴Howbeit many of them which heard the word believed; and the number of the men was about five thousand."* (Acts 4:1-4)

Notice how it **grieved** the "spiritual" authorities to see the disciples teaching the people and preaching the resurrection from the dead. Jebusites believe that "the people" are second-class spiritual citizens who don't deserve spiritual impartation because such freedom and potential is too "dangerous" in the hands of "plebeians". Jebusites believe that certain people should lie down on the ground and stay there. As we said above, they believe in the "killing" part, but not in the "resurrecting" part. They forget that the wheat is threshed in order to manifest the grain inside the husk, not to destroy the wheat:

"²³Give ye ear, and hear my voice; hearken, and hear my speech. ²⁴Doth the plowman plow all day to sow? doth he open and break the clods of his ground? ²⁵When he hath made plain the face thereof, doth he not cast abroad the fitches, and scatter the cummin, and cast in the principal wheat and the appointed barley and the rie in their place? ²⁶For his God doth instruct him to discretion, and doth teach him. ²⁷For the fitches are not threshed with a threshing instrument, neither is a cart wheel turned about upon the cummin; but the fitches are beaten out with a staff, and the cummin with a rod. ²⁸Bread corn is bruised; because he will not ever be threshing it, nor break it with the wheel of his cart, nor bruise it with his horsemen. ²⁹This also cometh forth from the LORD of hosts, which is wonderful in counsel, and excellent in working." (Isaiah 28:23-29)

The wheat is not to stay on the ground to be threshed forever (v28). After God produces **death** through His Word of Judgement, He unleashes **resurrection** power so that what was **sown** in death (the grain) may come to life:

"And that which thou sowest, thou sowest not that body that shall be, but bare grain, it may chance of wheat, or of some other grain:" (1 Corinthians 15:37)

35

As we see in the verse above, your life must be **sown** in order to be resurrected. If judgement comes on a person who refuses to hand over his or her life as a seed and who literally "holds on for dear life", God will have nothing to resurrect, because there can be no harvest where there is no seed:

"Whosoever shall seek to save his life shall lose it; and whosoever shall lose his life shall preserve it." (Luke 17:33)

An example of Godly rebellion

After the healing of the lame man, 5000 were converted to the Lord (Acts 4:4). The number "**5**" in Scripture is generally associated with "grace to minister"; this is why **5** ministries are listed in Ephesians 4:11 and why we have 5 fingers in each hand, since our hands are designed to serve or "minister" to others. On the other hand, the number "1000" in Scripture is generally associated with "abundance beyond measure". Therefore, since 5000 equals 5 times 1000, the 5000 converts are a prophetic figure of the abundance beyond measure of people to whom God wants to impart a grace to minister in these latter days. Whilst the Jebusites are out to restrict this grace to a select few, God is out to impart it to all of His people, and all those who are willing to receive it **will** receive this impartation, and there will be **many** who will receive it in these latter days.

Notice how the spiritual authorities of Peter and John's days reacted to the 5000 converts:

*"⁵And it came to pass on the morrow, that their rulers, and elders, and scribes, ⁶And Annas the high priest, and Caiaphas, and John, and Alexander, and as many as were of the kindred of the high priest, were gathered together at Jerusalem. ⁷And when they had set them in the midst, they asked, **By what power, or by what name, have ye done this?** ⁸Then Peter, filled with the Holy Ghost, said unto them, Ye rulers of the people, and elders of Israel," (Acts 4:5-8)*

As you can see in verse 7, Jebusites are always asking the "authorisation" question. In other words, they want to know, "**What recognised human leader authorised you to do this?**". Jebusites **demand** that believers seek "pastoral covering" to do things. I once heard a prophetess on TBN (a Christian television network) asking an audience at a spiritual conference if they had asked their pastors' permission to attend the conference. She then proceeded to tell everyone that, if they had not obtained that permission, they were in disobedience and would not receive God's blessing at the conference. What a stupid comment!!! It grieved my heart to hear such an anointed woman of God say such a foolish thing!!! As time has passed, I have seen how the Jebusite spirit has slowly drained the prophetic anointing from this woman's life. Jebusites prey on people's fear of "being in rebellion", and they have unfortunately been successful with this mighty woman of God. Prophets are **designed by God** to confront human authority; this is why prophets in the Old Testament constantly went before kings (anointed by **God** as kings) and challenged them with prophetic word from the Lord. Prophets are men and women who are not afraid to defy human structures. Prophets are the "*kamikaze*" corps in God's army. They are not afraid to die; they are not afraid to be stoned by the court of public opinion or to be executed by the ruling powers; therefore, they cannot be intimidated with death threats. When a prophet loses that fearless defiance of human structures, he or she becomes useless to God as a prophet. I have seen how the mighty woman of God I mentioned above continually beats up on (i.e.- "threshes") "regular" believers from the pulpit, but I have seen her literally kneeling in submission before a renowned pastor. A prophet of God must not be a respecter of persons. He or she must confront **everyone**'s iniquity, and must give his or her **unconditional** submission to no one but God, **even at the risk of appearing "rebellious" in the sight of natural man.**

In verse 8 of Acts 4 we find something most pastors prefer not to preach about. Peter, under the anointing of the Spirit, refers to the opponents of Christ as the "rulers of the people and the elders of Israel". In other words, he recognises these men as **valid authorities**. He then proceeds to confront them:

"*¹⁰Be it known unto you all, and to all the people of Israel, that by the name of Jesus Christ of Nazareth, **whom ye crucified**, whom God raised from the dead, even by him doth this man stand here before you whole. ¹¹This is the stone which was set at nought of you builders, which is become the head of the corner. ¹²Neither is there salvation in any other: for there is none other name under heaven given among men, whereby we must be saved. ¹³Now **when they saw the boldness of Peter and John**, and perceived that they were unlearned and ignorant men, they marvelled; and they took knowledge of them, that they had been with Jesus. ¹⁴And beholding the man which was healed standing with them, they could say nothing against it.*" (Acts 4:10-14)

Notice how Peter takes the opportunity in verse 10 to condemn the authorities as *murderers* of Christ when he says, "Jesus Christ of Nazareth, whom **ye crucified**". In verse 11, he declares them as "*lacking in spiritual discernment*" when he says that the stone that they have rejected has become God's cornerstone. In verse 12, *he rejects their names*, i.e.- their titles of "high priest", "elders", "rulers", and "scribes", declaring that those names do not bring salvation, since there is only one name which can redeem man's lost spiritual heritage: the name of Jesus. In other words, Peter answered their original question, "**What recognised human leader authorised you to do this?**" by saying,

> "No recognised human leader authorised us to do this. We are doing this in obedience to a Lord whom you cannot see with your natural eyes. We have no letter of recommendation from any authority you would recognise, and even if you had recognised Jesus as a human authority, He is not here in the flesh to prove to you that we have His covering. We follow an invisible name that is above any of your names, and we declare this despite the fact that we recognise you as legitimate rulers and elders of the people of Israel."

Verse 13 declares that these human leaders were stunned by the **boldness** of Peter and John. They were not used to "plebeians" speaking with the authority of the Spirit. Peter and John had no "covering" but the presence of God in their lives, and yet, these human leaders **refused** to believe in the message of these "unlearned" Galileans. They threatened them, ordering them (based on their human authority) not to speak at all or teach in the name of Jesus, but look at how Peter and John responded:

"[18]*And they called them, and commanded them not to speak at all nor teach in the name of Jesus.* [19]*But Peter and John answered and said unto them,* **Whether it be right in the sight of God to hearken unto you more than unto God, judge ye.** [20]*For we cannot but speak the things which we have seen and heard." (Acts 4:18-20)*

In other words, they said to the authorities,

> "We are **not** going to obey your orders, because we perceive in our spirits a message from God that is contrary to your human orders, and what God says to our hearts takes precedence over any human order, no matter whom that order comes from."

To make matters worse for any Jebusite reading these words, notice what the rest of the passage in Acts 4 declares:

"*[23]And being let go, they went to their own company, and reported all that the chief priests and elders had said unto them. [24]And when they heard that, they lifted up their voice to God with one accord, and said, Lord, thou art God, which hast made heaven, and earth, and the sea, and all that in them is: [25]Who by the mouth of **thy servant David** hast said, Why did the heathen rage, and the people imagine vain things? [26]The kings of the earth stood up, and the rulers were gathered together against the Lord, and against his Christ. [27]For of a truth against thy holy child Jesus, whom thou hast anointed, both Herod, and Pontius Pilate, with the Gentiles, and the people of Israel, were gathered together, [28]For to do whatsoever thy hand and thy counsel determined before to be done. [29]And now, Lord, behold their threatenings: and grant unto thy servants, that with all boldness they may speak thy word, [30]By stretching forth thine hand to heal; and that signs and wonders may be done by the name of thy holy child Jesus. [31]And when they had prayed, the place was shaken where they were assembled together; and they were all filled with the Holy Ghost, and they spake the word of God with boldness." (Acts 4:23-31)*

In verse 25, they refer to David as "God's servant", which is a term generally used in Scripture to refer to prophets, denoting their submission to God rather than to man:

"*[25]Since the day that your fathers came forth out of the land of Egypt unto this day I have even sent unto you all **my servants the prophets**, daily rising up early and sending them: [26]Yet they hearkened not unto me, nor inclined their ear, but hardened their neck: they did worse than their fathers." (Jeremiah 7:25-26)*

This means that David is being quoted in Acts 4:25-26 as a **prophet** submissive to God. Notice that these anointed believers quote Psalm 2:1-2, where David declares that the kings of the Earth and the rulers are gathered together against the Lord, and against His Anointed One. Doesn't this sound like a defiant condemnation of the authorities' actions? Aren't they saying that human authority is prone to acting in opposition to the anointing of the Spirit? Weren't human authorities the ones that crucified Christ when He was in the flesh? Just as they did with Christ 2000 years ago, religious authorities continue to "crucify" those who speak in the anointing of the Lord,

39

commanding them to submit to their human authority and structures. Pastors all over the world are quelling the prophetic voice of the Spirit in their congregations because they are more afraid of a declining membership than of being outside of God's will. God is tired of these men and women who are getting in the way of His mighty revival, and you will see, over the next 10 years, how mighty judgements will begin to be unleashed upon entire congregations, and even over entire cities and nations [these words were originally written in June 2004]. These judgements will tear down the cursed pastoral matriarchy[6] that has held the Church back from fulfilling its true prophetic calling. All you Jebusites who currently rule over Jerusalem, watch out, because **David is on his way**:

"[6]And **the king and his men went to Jerusalem unto the Jebusites**, *the inhabitants of the land: which spake unto David, saying, Except thou take away the blind and the lame, thou shalt not come in hither: thinking, David cannot come in hither. [7]Nevertheless **David took the strong hold of Zion**: the same is the city of David. [8]And David said on that day, Whosoever getteth up to the gutter, and smiteth the Jebusites, and the lame and the blind, that are hated of David's soul, he shall be chief and captain. Wherefore they said, The blind and the lame shall not come into the house. [9]So David dwelt in the fort, and called it the city of David. And David built round about from Millo and inward. [10]And David went on, and grew great, and the LORD God of hosts was with him." (2 Samuel 5:6-10)*
[The King James version mistranslated the middle part of verse 6. The original text says, "You shall not enter here, for even the blind and the lame will turn you away"]

Today's Jebusites are scornfully mocking God's prophetic remnant (today's "David"), saying that even the blind and the lame in Jerusalem can defeat David. Instead of being reprimanded by the Holy Spirit for defying human authority, the prophetic remnant (today's David) will receive God's confirmation in the same way that the believers of Acts 4 did. God will shake the earth (Acts 4:31), which represents the shaking of human structures in order to bring them down, and David will be filled with the Holy Spirit, which represents a mighty impartation of anointing upon God's prophetic remnant, causing them to speak the Word with even more boldness (Acts 4:31) against all human authority that dares to defy God's plans on the basis of its human titles and pedigree.

---

[6] You can read more on the "pastoral matriarchy" in the prophetic word titled "Bread in the sea" posted on the Shamah-Elim Bible Studies website (http://shamah-elim.info/p breadsea.htm).

So much more to say

There is a great deal more to say about the Jebusites. There is much to learn about the Jebusites as one studies the passage in 2 Samuel 24 that speaks of the threshing floor of "Arauna the Jebusite" (that threshing floor is a figure of today's Church). Many of the concepts we have studied here concerning the Jebusites are reaffirmed and expanded in this passage of Scripture.

The Jebusite spirit is under God's curse, and its days are numbered. May the God of Israel not find any reader of this book with a Jebusite spirit safely residing in his (her) heart when God's visitation comes upon him (her).

To learn more about the Jebusite spirit, we recommend the following postings from the Shamah-Elim Bible Studies website:

- Article "The stingy enemies of God"
  (http://shamah-elim.info/stgenemy.htm)
- Q & A word "The roots of homosexuality"
  (http://shamah-elim.info/qa/q_hmsx.htm)
- Article "The beginning of sorrows"
  (http://shamah-elim.info/bgnsorrw.htm)
- Prophetic word "Rain in Spain"
  (http://shamah-elim.info/p_spainrn.htm)
- Prophetic word "Katrina is hard on Big Easy (Part 8)"
  (http://shamah-elim.info/p_katrina8.htm)

The Jebusite spirit is better understood in the context of its interaction with the Amorite spirit, which we study in the next chapter.

Chapter 3
The Amorites

This chapter will focus on the "Amorites". Wherever there are Jebusites, there will always be an Amorite whose will the Jebusites will enforce. Amorites also help Girgashites to have a sense of "stability" and "belonging". Girgashites generally stay out of the way of the strong Amorites, due to the Girgashites' deeply-rooted fear of death.

An article similar to this chapter is posted on the Shamah-Elim Bible Studies website at the following web address:
http://shamah-elim.info/amorite.htm

What's in a name?

A great deal can be inferred directly from the meaning of the word "Amorite". The name "Amorite" literally means, "mountain people; renowned". Since mountains refer to tall and impressive land masses that dominate over valleys, we can infer that the Amorite spirit is a spirit of **self-exaltation**. The word for Amorite in Hebrew comes from another Hebrew word, *amar*, which means, "to utter, to say"; this implies that people with Amorite spirits are people who **want their name uttered** or mentioned. Amorites are **fame-seekers**, seekers of human glory and greatness. Practically all dictators in history are Amorites. People like Saddam Hussein, Fidel Castro, Adolph Hitler, and Joseph Stalin, who like to dominate and control others, who love to see pictures of themselves plastered all over entire cities and countries, and who love to see their subjects revere and worship them, are men whose hearts are possessed by Amorite spirits.

Just as mountains tend to dominate over the landscape they are in, Amorites are people who like to dominate and rule over others. They tend to establish an imposing and seemingly immovable presence.

"*19Then came the disciples to Jesus apart, and said, Why could not we cast him out? 20And Jesus said unto them, Because of your unbelief: for verily I say unto you, If ye have faith as a grain of mustard seed, **ye shall say unto this mountain, Remove hence to yonder place; and it shall remove**; and nothing shall be impossible unto you.*" (Matthew 17:19-20)

When the Lord talks about us removing mountains, He was not simply talking about "big problems", as most preachers teach. He was talking about the uprooting of spiritual powers in high places. Instead of focusing our faith on getting things from God, our faith is to focus on the tearing down of principalities and powers that get in the way of God's kingdom being established on Earth. We are soldiers in a battle to take back the Earth for God, and, as soldiers, we are not here to please ourselves but to execute the orders of our Commander-In-Chief, the Lord Jesus Christ. This "taking back of the Earth" from the Amorites who dominate it is not to be done through human means, but through the activation of faith that is apparently small in comparison to these spirits, but which has the dynamite potential to overtake them. This is because our faith is a seed with **kingdom potential** in it. You and I, my brother and sister, have the potential to establish God's kingdom on Earth. **All** believers have the capability to tear down Amorite spirits from the heavens.

"What say you, oh king"?

As we said above, the Hebrew word for "Amorite" comes from another Hebrew word meaning, "to say, to utter". Besides referring to the Amorites' zest for publicity (i.e.- their zest for hearing their name uttered and revered by others), this also implies that Amorites love to "say", and have people "obey". The word "Amorite" could literally be translated as "sayer". Amorites long to be like ancient Roman emperors who simply give out orders and have people moving heaven and earth to get those orders fulfilled. In other words, Amorites love to be "**kings**".

As we shared in this book's introductory overview, Deuteronomy 7:1 lists the 7 types of evil spirits we are to war against; they are the Hittites, the Girgashites, the Amorites, the Canaanites, the Perizzites, the Hivites, and the Jebusites. When doing a computer search of the Old Testament verses that contain any of these 7 names in Hebrew along with the Hebrew word for king, *melek*, interesting results appear:

# of Verses	Verses referring specifically to...
23	Amorite kings
2	Amorite and Canaanite kings
3	Canaanite kings
3	Hittite kings
1	Kings of all 7 nations except for the Girgashites

Notice how this verse count is dominated by the Amorites, confirming the fact that the Holy Spirit relates the Amorite spirits with **earthly kings** that try to get in the way of **His** Kingship. Amorites see God as their competition. Since they want subjects who obey anything they say, Amorites resent subjects who disobey their commands and who claim to have heard the voice of God giving them a different command:

"*17But that it spread no further among the people, let us straitly threaten them, that they speak henceforth to no man in this name. 18And **they called them, and commanded them not to speak at all nor teach** in the name of Jesus. 19But Peter and John answered and said unto them, **Whether it be right in the sight of God to hearken unto you more than unto God**, judge ye. 20For we cannot but speak the things which we have seen and heard." (Acts 4:17-20)*

As we saw in the previous chapter[7], the Jebusites in the Body of Christ want to prevent God's people speaking. They prefer spiritually lame believers who have no spiritual authority and who will never dare to question the "rulings" decreed by authorities. Jebusites, therefore, become the Amorite's "right-hand men". Jebusites are the police, the enforcers of the Amorite king's laws. A clear example of this appears in the following passage:

"*19The high priest then asked Jesus of his disciples, and of his doctrine. 20Jesus answered him, I spake openly to the world; I ever taught in the synagogue, and in the temple, whither the Jews always resort; and in secret have I said nothing. 21**Why askest thou me?** ask them which heard me, what I have said unto them: behold, they know what I said. 22And **when he had thus spoken, one of the officers which stood by struck Jesus with the palm of his hand, saying, Answerest thou the high priest so?** 23Jesus answered him, If I have spoken evil, bear witness of the evil: but if well, why smitest thou me?"* (John 18:19-23)

In Jesus's days, the high priest, a legitimate spiritual authority, was revered by religious people. No self-respecting religious Jew would dare to question anything the high priest said. When Jesus challenged the high priest's questioning in verse 21, one of the priest's officers struck Jesus in the face with the palm of his hand as if to say,

---

[7] pg. 33

"How dare you question my Amorite king's orders? You are a nobody compared to him. Just shut up. Stop 'expressing yourself' and answer what the priest specifically asked you."

Here, the officer was under the influence of a Jebusite spirit whilst the high priest exerted an Amorite influence of kingly domination over the religious people of those days.

Notice how the Amorite spirit can manifest itself through a real authority who is holding a position established by God Himself. In John 18:19, the priest before which Jesus stood is called "high priest" by the Holy Spirit, and the office of "high priest" was an office instituted by God Himself (Leviticus 21:10). God bestows authority upon a person, but he or she has the prerogative to either exercise that authority under God's anointing or to exercise it in his or her flesh. When that authority promotes God's will, it spreads God's **king**dom. When it promotes man's will, it spreads the kingdom of an Amorite. You and I have been equipped with the mind of the Anointed One (1 Corinthians 2:15-16) and are called to discern which kingdom is being spread; once we have discerned, we must act accordingly.

How are you using your palms?

In the section above, we saw how a Jebusite, an officer of the high priest, struck Jesus with the palm of his hand. Why the "palm of his hand"? To answer this, we have to go to the Old Testament. The Hebrew word used in the Old Testament for "palm" is *kaph*, which can refer to the palm of the hand or to the sole of the foot; in fact, *kaph* is translated as "sole" in many verses. Therefore, the officer striking Jesus with his "*kaph*" is a prophetic figure of how the officer was trying to "stomp on Jesus's face" with the "sole of his feet", so to speak, just like a (Jebusite) thresher trampling over wheat.

The word *kaph* comes from another Hebrew word, *kaphaph*, which means "to bend down, to bow down", in reference to the palm's ability to bend, as when you close your hand. Therefore, when the officer struck Jesus with the palm of his hand, he was ordering Jesus to "**bow down**", to "submit" to the Amorite's commands.

The "palm" also conveys another message, which can be found when we study a relatively obscure passage in Deuteronomy:

"[11]When men strive together one with another, and the wife of the one draweth near for to deliver her husband out of the hand of him that smiteth him, and putteth forth her hand, and taketh

him by the secrets: ¹²Then thou shalt cut off her hand, thine eye shall not pity her." (Deuteronomy 25:11-12)

The word translated as "hand" in verse 12 is the Hebrew word *kaph* mentioned above, meaning that, in Hebrew, verse 12 literally says, "Then you shall cut off her palm". When we match this passage up against John 18:19-23, we can see that the "husband" corresponds to the high priest, the "wife" corresponds to the officer, and the other man corresponds to Jesus. Many believers (under the influence of Jebusite spirits) act like zealous wives protective of their husbands, lashing out at anyone who dares to say anything that questions the pastor's "greatness" or authority.

The word for "secrets" at the end of Deuteronomy 25:11 is the Hebrew word *mabush*, which refers to a man's private parts. Literally, *mabush* means "that which provokes shame", and comes from another word, *buwsh*, which means "to put to shame". Therefore, when Jebusite believers use their palms to strike those who speak in Jesus but who have no "religious title" to support their words, they are seeking **to provoke shame**, to humiliate the other person, but it is a flesh-induced shame, not a Spirit-induced shame, since it is generally based on a comparison of human titles. To the high priest officer of John 18, Jesus was a nobody; He was not even a Levite, so He could not aspire to "priesthood" under the covenant that was in place at the time. Annas, however, was **the** "high priest", the priest above all priests, the highest spiritual authority recognised by the people. The officer would turn to the high priest, and he would see a man robed in elegant high priest attire; he would then turn to Jesus, and see an "itinerant preacher" from Galilee, of all places; and, who ever heard of a prophet coming out of Galilee (John 7:52)? Besides, this "preacher" was now a prisoner. It was "obvious" to the officer which of the two was the greater individual, so the officer proceeded to slap Jesus in the face with his palm and ask, "How dare you talk back to the **high priest**? Shame on you!!" (John 18:22). Jebusites protect their Amorite pastors from believers who are speaking under the prophetic anointing by telling the believer to compare his or her human titles to the pastor's human titles, and, most of the time, if not always, the Amorite pastor will win this comparison.

Throughout Scripture, whenever a distinction is made between "*man*" and "*woman*" in a given passage, "man" will generally refer to a **spirit** and "woman" will refer to a **soul**. This is not to say that women are not spirits, but is to say that, in their husband-wife relationship, women have a "soul" role whilst men have a "spirit" role. When a woman is in her "wife" role, she must be submissive to her husband, in the same way that a soul must always be submissive to God's Spirit. When a woman steps outside of her **role** as "wife", she can, at **any** given moment, speak under the anointing of the Spirit and give a word of the Lord to her husband which he **must submit** to, because, in the Anointed One, there is no "man or woman", the Bible declares (Galatians 3:27-28). Being a "wife", therefore, is a **role** a woman plays. If she lives in submission to the Spirit, she will know when she is to put on the hat that says "wife" and when she is to put on the hat that says "**son** of God" (Luke 20:34-36). Having said all of this, we emphasise once again that, in Scripture, passages that distinguish between "man" and "woman" are portraying prophetic figures of spirits versus souls.

Therefore, when Deuteronomy 25:11 speaks about the wife taking the "private parts" of her husband's attacker with her hand, the Word is referring to a soul questioning the attacker's "**manhood**", i.e.- his **spiritual** authority. Whenever Jebusites tell prophets to shut up, they are saying,

> "You are not a spirit; you are a mere soul, and, as a soul you must submit to the authority of the Amorite because he is a spirit, and you are just a soul"

This is why so many male and female believers are deprived of their spiritual "manhood" (I am speaking in the Spirit), and live as submissive souls, never becoming aware of their spiritual authority in Christ, the Anointed One. Amorites make a concerted effort to remove your awareness of that spiritual authority, because they want your unconditional faithfulness. They want you to see them as the king, the one whose sovereign will **must** be fulfilled. Since the will resides in the heart, they want to control your heart, making every effort possible to prevent your heart hearing God's voice directly. Amorite pastors, with the help of their Jebusite officers, love to preach the following:

> "I will hear the voice of God for you. That's what I am here for. You just submit to my authority, obey everything I say, and you will be OK with God. You desperately need my covering and approval, because, without it, you are in rebellion, and God will not bless your life. Don't ever, ever go to God directly and ask him if what I said is from him or not. There are many spirits of deceit out there, and you might just hear one of those spirits and think it is God speaking to you. You are not equipped to hear God's voice. John 10:27 is not true. Leave all that 'discerning' stuff up to me. Let me be your hero. Let me be your king."

Another spiritual interpretation for the word for palm in Hebrew (*kaph*) can be seen through the following passages:

"Doth not Hezekiah persuade you to give over yourselves to die by famine and by thirst, saying, The LORD our God shall deliver us out of the hand of the king of Assyria?" (2 Chronicles 32:11)

The word translated as "hand" in the passage above is the Hebrew word *kaph* once again, so the final part of the verse should really say, "The LORD our God shall deliver us out of the **palm** of the king of Assyria". Since the palm is the hollow, inner part of the hand, to be in a king's palm means to be in his grasp, or **to be under his total control**. When the officer struck Jesus in John 18:22, he was telling Jesus, "I am under this man's total control, and so should you; submit yourself to him!!".

Another passage where the Hebrew word for palm is used to speak about being under someone's total control is the following:

"And I will deliver thee out of the hand of the wicked, and I will redeem thee out of the hand of the terrible." (Jeremiah 15:21)

Again, the word "hand" used in the phrase "hand of the terrible" above is from the Hebrew word for palm, *kaph*. The word translated as "terrible" is the Hebrew word *ariyts*, which is derived from the word *arats*, meaning, "to tremble, to fear, to oppress". Amorites love to oppress and to create a sense of dread and fear in the people they want to rule over. If there is any doubt, just consider those who have lived under the oppression of Amorites such as Fidel Castro or Saddam Hussein. It is interesting to note, however, that many people who live under Amorite domination become so accustomed to the Amorite's reign of terror that they often speak in favour of their oppressive leaders, rarely saying anything negative against them. Through the help of the Jebusites, the Amorites brainwash people into actually thinking that it is a **sin** to say anything that confronts the Amorite leader.

So far, we have seen how Jebusites strike others with their palms as an "act of stomping"; it is a command to "bow down" to the Amorite, and it is an act intended to provoke shame and to question the other person's spirit authority. The palm also represents being under the Amorite king's total control. My beloved brother and sister in Christ, is there blood in your palms? Have you ever unknowingly struck a son of God in the face because he or she dared to question "your" pastor's commands or viewpoints?

*"³For **your hands are defiled with blood**, and your fingers with iniquity; your lips have spoken lies, your tongue hath muttered perverseness ... ⁷Their feet run to evil, and they make haste to shed innocent blood: their thoughts are thoughts of iniquity; wasting and destruction are in their paths." (Isaiah 59:3,7)*

[The word translated as "hands" in verse 3 is *kaph*, once again.]

If there is innocent blood in your palms, God wants you to repent, and if you do, God will wipe the innocent blood of His son from your hands, and He will release you from that Amorite-defending, Jebusite spirit that has established itself in your heart. God did it with Saul of Tarsus (Acts 7:54-8:3, 9:1-9). He can do it with you. He wants to do mighty things through you, just as He did with Saul of Tarsus, but you must be willing to recognise **Him** as your only **King**, the only One deserving of your **unconditional submission and loyalty**. Don't let any Amorite take God's place in your heart, even if that Amorite has the title of "Pastor", "Prophet", "Apostle", "Bishop", "Reverend", "pope", etc.

Don't let the cock crow on you

Before the events that took place in John chapter 18, the Lord gives Simon Peter the following prophetic word:

"Jesus answered him, Wilt thou lay down thy life for my sake? Verily, verily, I say unto thee, The cock shall not crow, till thou hast denied me thrice." (John 13:38)

Why did the Lord use a cock's crowing to confirm Simon Peter's denials? To answer this, we need to observe a cock's behaviour. I have always been a city person, but I have heard (from people who have owned chickens) that cocks usually establish dominion over a "harem" of female chickens. From what I have heard, a cock can get very jealous and aggressive when another cock invades its territory, and it usually fights against any intruding cock to drive it away from its "girls". In other words, cocks want to be "kings of their territory", and they get very aggressive when any "intruder" comes to put its domination into question. The "chicks" are his, and no one better try to take them away from him!! This is why cocks are a perfect example of the Amorite spirit. Amorites are territorial spirits who like to dominate over great numbers of souls, seeing them as trophies of their "greatness", and people who have Amorite spirits in their hearts exhibit this exact behaviour. The territorial nature of the Amorites is emphasised by the following passage:

"²¹*And Israel sent messengers unto **Sihon king of the Amorites**, saying, ²²Let me pass through thy land: we will not turn into the fields, or into the vineyards; we will not drink of the waters of the well: but we will go along by the king's high way, until we be past thy borders. ²³And **Sihon would not suffer Israel to pass through his border**: but Sihon gathered all his people together, and went out against Israel into the wilderness: and he came to Jahaz, and fought against Israel." (Numbers 21:21-23)*

[Paraphrasing, Sihon king of the Amorites said to Israel: "Don't come near my property, or I'll shoot!!".]

When they are agitated, cocks can flare their neck feathers as they crow to form something resembling a "crown" or "wreath" around their necks. This is a way of saying, "Hey, I am lord and master of this territory!! I am top dog here!!". As one studies John chapter 18 carefully, it becomes evident that the Amorite spirits were agitatedly crowing the night that Jesus was arrested:

"¹⁵*And Simon Peter followed Jesus, and so did another disciple: that disciple was known unto the high priest, and went in with Jesus into the palace of the high priest. ¹⁶But Peter stood at the door without. Then went out that other disciple, which was known unto the high priest, and spake unto **her that kept the door**, and brought in Peter. ¹⁷Then saith the damsel that kept the door unto Peter, Art not thou also one of this man's disciples? He saith, I am not. ¹⁸And **the servants and officers stood there**, who had made a fire of coals; for it was cold: and they warmed themselves: and Peter stood with them, and warmed himself." (John 18:15-18)*

Notice that, in his first denial, Simon Peter is inside the high priest's palace. Simon Peter had entered the cock's territory. Annas, the high priest, was an Amorite, and one of his servile subjects, the young lady who kept guard at the door (v17), confronted Simon Peter about being one of Jesus's disciples. In spiritual terms, the young lady, under a Jebusite influence, was asking Simon,

"Chicken, what cock do you belong to? You don't belong to that cock called Jesus of Nazareth, do you? Just look at what my cock, the high priest, is doing to that cock!!"

Notice how verse 18 emphasises the "servants and the officers", all of them servile subjects of the Amorite high priest. The warmth of the "fire of coals" represents the covering and protection that Amorites offer their subjects. "**Without me**", the Amorites say, "**you'll be out in** the cold!! Come and put yourself under my protection. Just give me your unconditional loyalty, and I'll take care of you! Just throw your apostolic calling in the fire the same way everyone else already has. That serves as more coal for my fire!!"

Simon threw his **apostolic** calling here because the one questioning him was the servant who "kept the door". Doors or gates in Scripture are symbolic of judgement, because judgements in ancient cities were performed at the gates, and the ministry most related to "word of judgement" is the apostolic ministry, since the **apostolic anointing** is to endow the Church with wisdom (1 Corinthians 2:1 and 2:7, Colossians 1:1, and 1:28-1:29), and wisdom is given by God to execute judgements (1 Kings 3:9-12).

In Simon's second and third denials, the cock strikes again:

"^{24}Now Annas had sent him bound unto Caiaphas the high priest. ^{25}And Simon Peter stood and warmed himself. They said therefore unto him, Art not thou also one of his disciples? He denied it, and said, I am not. ^{26}**One of the servants of the high priest**, being his kinsman whose ear Peter cut off, saith, Did not I see thee in **the garden** with him? ^{27}Peter then denied again: and immediately the cock crew." (John 18:24-27)

From one Amorite high priest, Annas, Jesus was sent to another Amorite high priest, Caiaphas (there were two high priests at the time, according to Luke 3:2). As this happened, the chickens of Caiaphas the cock got on Simon Peter's case once again, asking him if he was one of Jesus's "chickens". When Simon Peter denied being a disciple of Jesus, he cast the **prophetic anointing** on his life into the fire. This can be said for two reasons. One is the fact that Annas and Caiaphas were co-high priests, and, as we saw above, Simon's first denial was at the price of his apostolic calling; since the apostolic and the prophetic anointing generally work together (Ephesians 2:20), we can infer that the denial whilst Jesus was with Caiaphas cost Peter his prophetic anointing. A second reason is because the word translated as "stood" in John 18:25 is from a Greek word literally meaning "**was**"; this means, therefore, that verse 25 referred to Simon Peter's **presence** there. In Scripture, the ministry most related to the manifestation and the fullness of God's presence is the prophetic ministry, since the prophetic anointing removes the void in people's lives, giving them a sense of purpose and calling; in other words, the prophetic anointing brings the fullness of God's presence into people's lives.

Peter's third denial, in John 18:27, cost him the **evangelistic anointing** on his life. Why? Because the one confronting him asked him if he had been with Jesus at the **garden** (v26). The garden speaks of a place with "earth"; this points to the Girgashite spirit, which we studied in chapter 1. A close study of Luke 5:1-11 and other passages reveals that Simon the fisherman was a man under a strong Girgashite influence in his life. In fact, Simon's evangelistic calling as a "fisher of men" was revealed to him (Luke 5:11) only until that Girgashite influence was broken by Jesus (Luke 5:1-10). Simon had been a practical businessman all of his life, and it was only when Jesus broke this Girgashite practicality that Simon woke up to the higher calling in his life, which was to be a mighty evangelist of God. When the servile Girgashite of John 18:27 confronted Simon about being in the garden, he was, in a spiritual sense, reminding him of his "Girgashite roots", thereby calling him to resign from the "lofty ambition" of being a mighty evangelist for the Lord.

Notice how Simon Peter's denials were all spawned by conversations with **servants**. There was a **spirit of servility** in the air that night, and that spirit drained Simon Peter from his apostolic, prophetic, and evangelistic anointing. As we share in an article posted on the Shamah-Elim Bible Studies website[8], the apostolic, the prophetic, and the evangelistic ministries are the 3 "male" ministries, whilst the pastor and teacher ministries are the 2 "female" ministries (here, we are using the terms "male" and "female" in a figurative sense). Therefore, when Simon Peter was drained of his apostolic, prophetic, and evangelistic anointings, he was, in effect, deprived of his "**spiritual manhood**", so to speak, and was reduced to a mere "female" **soul**, a scared soul that would die without the warmth and covering of some Amorite spirit. When we allow Amorite spirits to crow on us, we are drained from **our authority as spirits**, and become mere souls that differ little from animals, since animals also have souls (but no spirit). When you are deprived of your spirit authority, you are deprived of your "humanity"; i.e.- you are deprived of what truly makes you unique and different from animals and all other created beings in the physical realm. Don't let the cock crow on you.

---

[8] The article is titled "Male and female ministries" (http://shamah-elim.info/mfmin.htm).

Malchus the servant

In John 18:10, as Jesus was about to be arrested by the mob of chief priest officers (i.e.- the Amorites' Jebusites), Simon Peter did the following:

*"10Then Simon Peter having a sword drew it, and **smote the high priest's servant**, and **cut off his right ear**. The servant's name was Malchus." (John 18:10)*

Why did Simon Peter cut off the **right ear**? Some might say, "Well, he was a fisherman, not a soldier, so his aim with the sword was not that good!!" I might take that answer if we were looking at this passage from a natural perspective, but, since the Holy Spirit took the time to remind John to write down which ear it was, we must be certain that God is trying to tell us something. **All** things that happen in the material world are consequences of things happening in the spirit world. To quote the singer Sting, *"We are spirits in the material world"*.

The ear obviously refers to the act of hearing, and hearing, in Scripture, is very much related to the concept of **obeying** someone's orders. You cannot be a good waiter, for example, if you do not listen carefully to the client's order. You cannot be a good employee if you don't listen carefully to your boss's orders. You cannot be a good slave if you don't listen carefully to your master's orders:

*"Hearken unto me, my people; and **give ear unto me**, O my nation: for a law shall proceed from me, and I will make my judgment to rest for a light of the people." (Isaiah 51:4)*

*"And Moses called all Israel, and said unto them, Hear, O Israel, the **statutes and judgments which I speak in your ears** this day, **that ye may** learn them, and keep, and **do them**." (Deuteronomy 5:1)*

"12And if thy brother, an Hebrew man, or an Hebrew woman, be sold unto thee, and serve thee six years; then in the seventh year thou shalt let him go free from thee. 13And when thou sendest him out free from thee, thou shalt not let him go away empty: 14Thou shalt furnish him liberally out of thy flock, and out of thy floor, and out of thy winepress: of that wherewith the LORD thy God hath blessed thee thou shalt give unto him. 15And thou shalt remember that thou wast a bondman in the land of

*Egypt, and the LORD thy God redeemed thee: therefore I command thee this thing to day. ¹⁶And it shall be, if he say unto thee, I will not go away from thee; because he loveth thee and thine house, because he is well with thee; ¹⁷Then **thou shalt take an aul, and thrust it through his ear unto the door, and he shall be thy servant for ever**. And also unto thy maidservant thou shalt do likewise. ¹⁸It shall not seem hard unto thee, when thou sendest him away free from thee; for he hath been worth a double hired servant to thee, in serving thee six years: and the LORD thy God shall bless thee in all that thou doest." (Deuteronomy 15:12-18)*

Notice how the sign of permanent "slavery" was made by piercing the slave's **ear** against the door (Deuteronomy 15:17). When Simon Peter cut off the servant's right ear, it is as if he was trying to free the servant from his slavery to his Amorite master, from his having to hear and obey his Amorite lord. It's like going to the zoo and opening the zebra's cage and telling the zebra to "go, go, run and be free like the wind". This "zebra", however, did not want to leave the cage. Malchus the servant was comfortable in his state of slavery, in his state of dependency to his Amorite master. This is why Jesus restored his ear, as a sign that Malchus did not want to be free, and as a sign to Simon Peter that he was trying to do things the wrong way.

The fact that Simon Peter cut off the **right** ear, as opposed to the left ear, is because the "right" side is generally related in Scripture to the establishment of authority:

*"¹ The LORD said unto my Lord, Sit thou **at my right hand**, until I make thine enemies thy footstool. ²The LORD shall send the rod of thy strength out of Zion: rule thou in the midst of thine enemies. ³Thy people shall be willing in the day of thy power, in the beauties of holiness from the womb of the morning: thou hast the dew of thy youth. ⁴The LORD hath sworn, and will not repent, Thou art a priest for ever after the order of Melchizedek. ⁵**The Lord at thy right hand** shall strike through kings in the day of his wrath. ⁶**He shall judge among the heathen**, he shall fill the places with the dead bodies; he shall wound the heads over many countries. ⁷He shall drink of the brook in the way: therefore shall he lift up the head." (Psalm 110:1-7)*

By cutting off Malchus' **right** ear, it is as if Simon Peter was saying to Malchus: "Don't listen anymore to that authority you have yielded your heart to. Yield your heart to the invisible authority of Jesus, not to the visible authority of the high priest". Even though Simon Peter's idea was right, his method was wrong. The Malchuses of this world cannot be set free from their self-imposed slavery through human means.

As shown by Psalm 110 quoted above, Jesus is a priest "after the order of Melchisedec" (Psalm 110:4, Hebrews 5:6). This type of priesthood is **not discernable with the natural eye**, as opposed to the priesthood after the order of Aaron, which is the priesthood that Caiaphas and Ananias belonged to. Malchus was following the Aaronic high priest because that priesthood was visible to the natural eye, and he rejected the Melchisedec high priest (i.e.- Jesus) because His authority was not naturally visible. Notice, however, that those who abide in the Melchisedec priesthood will be the ones who strike down earthly kings (Psalm 110:5).

Ironically, Malchus means "king", since it is the Greek version of the Hebrew word *melek* mentioned at the beginning of this chapter[9]. "Malchus the servant", therefore, is a contradiction in terms. Malchus is a figure of so many believers who have not woken up to the awareness that they are **spiritual kings** (Revelation 1:6, 2:26, 3:21), **mighty spirit beings, strong conquerors** called to take the spiritual atmosphere back from satan so that God's kingdom may be established. We have the name of a king, but act and live like servants. We are mighty spiritual beings who are called to manifest God's power and glory, but we have resigned ourselves to living comfortable earthly lives under the warmth and covering of Amorite cocks that happily enclose us in their "chicken harems".

"*[12]Be astonished, O ye heavens, at this, and be horribly afraid, be ye very desolate, saith the LORD. [13]For my people have committed two evils; they have forsaken me the fountain of living waters, and hewed them out cisterns, broken cisterns, that can hold no water. [14]Is Israel a servant? is he a homeborn slave? Why is he spoiled? [15]The young lions roared upon him, and yelled, and they made his land waste: his cities are burned without inhabitant." (Jeremiah 2:12-15)*
    [The word "spoiled" at the end of verse 14 should really say "taken as spoils". Amorites love to take spoils.]

As a prophetic figure, Simon Peter, in his Girgashite earthliness, tried to free Malchus through human means, but the "Malchus Church" can only be freed through men and women who, like the Lord

---

[9] pg. 43

Jesus, are willing to die. Amorite cocks always threaten "non-submissive chickens" with death. This "death" can take many forms. For example, I have heard some Amorite pastors preach the following: "If you do not submit to your local church authorities, you will be left behind at the time of the rapture". Others preach, "If you do not ask for my covering to attend that spiritual conference, God will not bless you there". Others preach, "If you do not obey your pastor's orders, God will not prosper your business". All of these are different ways of saying, "If you don't submit to me, you will die". It is, therefore, those who are willing to die that become the "liberators of the Malchuses". Since they can't be intimidated with death, the Amorites cannot use death as a weapon to stop them speaking. Even when the Amorites do kill these liberators, as they did with Jesus, their spiritual resistance cannot be annulled, since their blood cries out from the ground to God and unleashes God's righteous indignation on the Amorites. This is the reason why the earth trembled when Jesus died, and many who were prisoners in their sepulchres were set free at that moment:

"*50 Jesus, when he had cried again with a loud voice, yielded up the ghost. 51And, behold, the veil of the temple was rent in twain from the top to the bottom; and the earth did quake, and the rocks rent; 52And the graves were opened; and many bodies of the saints which slept arose, 53And **came out of the graves** after his resurrection, and went into the holy city, and appeared unto many." (Matthew 27:50-53).*

By killing the liberators, Amorites seal their own demise. Unfortunately, not many are willing to lay down their lives (literally or figuratively) in order to see the Malchuses liberated. I hope, my brother and sister in Christ, that you are one of those liberators.

So much more to say

There is so much more to say concerning the Amorites!!! There is much prophetic Word in Scripture that declares God's judgements against these spirits and against those who harbour them in their hearts. The lameness and muteness that the Amorites, the Jebusites, and the Girgashites have imposed on the Church shall be broken, and God's glory **shall** be seen in His house:

"*1**Behold, a king shall reign in righteousness**, and princes shall rule in judgment. 2And a man shall be as an hiding place from the wind, and a covert from the tempest; as rivers of water in a dry place, as the shadow of a great rock in a weary land.*

³**And the eyes of them that see shall not be dim,** and **the ears of them that hear shall hearken**. ⁴**The heart also of the rash shall understand knowledge**, and **the tongue of the stammerers shall be ready to speak plainly**. ⁵The vile person shall be no more called liberal, nor the churl said to be bountiful. ⁶For the vile person will speak villany, and his heart will work iniquity, to practise hypocrisy, and to utter error against the LORD, to make empty the soul of the hungry, and he will cause the drink of the thirsty to fail. ⁷The instruments also of the churl are evil: he deviseth wicked devices to destroy the poor with lying words, even when the needy speaketh right. ⁸But the liberal deviseth liberal things; and by liberal things shall he stand. ⁹Rise up, ye women that are at ease; hear my voice, ye careless daughters; give ear unto my speech. ¹⁰Many days and years shall ye be troubled, ye careless women: for the vintage shall fail, the gathering shall not come. ¹¹Tremble, ye women that are at ease; be troubled, ye careless ones: strip you, and make you bare, and gird sackcloth upon your loins. ¹²They shall lament for the teats, for the pleasant fields, for the fruitful vine. ¹³Upon the land of my people shall come up thorns and briers; yea, upon all the houses of joy in the joyous city: ¹⁴Because the palaces shall be forsaken; the multitude of the city shall be left; the forts and towers shall be for dens for ever, a joy of wild asses, a pasture of flocks; ¹⁵Until the spirit be poured upon us from on high, and the wilderness be a fruitful field, and the fruitful field be counted for a forest" (Isaiah 32:1-15)

"⁵**For he bringeth down them that dwell on high; the lofty city, he layeth it low; he layeth it low, even to the ground;** he bringeth it even to the dust. ⁶**The foot shall tread it down, even the feet of the poor**, and the steps of the needy. ⁷The way of the just is uprightness: thou, most upright, dost weigh the path of the just. ⁸Yea, in the way of thy judgments, O LORD, have we waited for thee; the desire of our soul is to thy name, and to the remembrance of thee. ⁹With my soul have I desired thee in the night; yea, with my spirit within me will I seek thee early: for when thy judgments are in the earth, the inhabitants of the world will learn righteousness. ¹⁰Let favour be shewed to the wicked, yet will he not learn righteousness: in the land of uprightness will he deal unjustly, and will not behold the majesty of the LORD. ¹¹LORD, when thy hand is lifted up, they will not see: but they shall see, and be ashamed for their envy at the people; yea, the fire of thine enemies shall devour them" (Isaiah 26:5-11)

To learn more about the Amorite spirit and "spiritual malehood", we recommend the following postings from the Shamah-Elim Bible Studies website:

- Article "Male and female ministries"
  (http://shamah-elim.info/mfmin.htm)
- Article "The Tyre treason"
  (http://shamah-elim.info/tyretrsn.htm)
- Article "The beginning of sorrows"
  (http://shamah-elim.info/bgnsorrw.htm)
- Prophetic word "Shame removed"
  (http://shamah-elim.info/p_shamermv.htm)
- Prophetic word "The 4 leviathans"
  (http://shamah-elim.info/p_4leviath.htm)
- Prophetic word "Flight 358"
  (http://shamah-elim.info/p_flite358.htm)
- Question & Answer "Dog-eating bears"
  (http://shamah-elim.info/qa/q_bear.htm)

Chapter 4
The Hittites

This chapter will focus on the "Hittites", the most invisible and most deceiving type of spirit. Interestingly enough, it is the spirit with the most "spiritual" manifestations, which contrasts with the Girgashites' more "down-to-earth" manifestation.

An article similar to this chapter is posted on the Shamah-Elim Bible Studies website at the following web address:
http://shamah-elim.info/hittite.htm

What's in a name?

A great deal can be inferred directly from the meaning of the word "Hittite", which literally means, "sons of terror". The Hittites were descendants of Heth, whose name means "terror". The word "terror" refers to an extreme manifestation of fear, and is always related to an element of **mystery**. For example, you may be afraid of a live wire because you **know** that enough electricity is running through it so as to hurt you if you touch it; this, however, does not qualify as "terror". Terror is when you are walking down a dark alley at night and you **don't know** if someone is about to leap out from either side and attack you. Terror is when you have heard that a serial killer has been attacking in your neighbourhood and you don't know if your house is his next target. Since terror is related to the unknown, it has to do with things that your mind cannot see. Out of the 3 components of the soul[10], the mind is the component that acts and reasons based on what it can see or perceive, whereas the heart is the component that hears, using the emotions as its "hearing antennas". Therefore, we can say that terror is **more emotional than mental**, and is based more on what your emotions **hear** than on what your mind can see.

Hittites, being spirits of terror, are **stealth operators** that attack the emotions and are the spirits behind nightmares and non-rational phobias such as claustrophobia, agoraphobia, exaggerated fear of dogs, and fear of being in the dark. As anyone who has suffered

---

[10] You can read more on the 3 components of the soul (the mind, the emotions, and the heart) in the article "Male and female ministries", under the section "The role of pastors and teachers" (http://shamah-elim.info/mfmin.htm), and the article "3 levels of pastoring" (http://shamah-elim.info/3lvlpast.htm) posted on the Shamah-Elim Bible Studies website.

from a phobia can testify, terror produces a sense of **deep emotional despair and torment**, and it causes a desire not to live anymore. Hittite spirits, therefore, are also behind **suicides** (this explains why terrorist groups such as Al-Qaeda and Hamas -- God curse them -- drive their followers to commit suicide). My dear friend, if you are undergoing deep emotional despair, and suicidal thoughts are haunting you, you are being attacked by Hittite spirits. I don't know if this serves as a consolation to you, but prophets in Scripture were constantly attacked by Hittite spirits. A strong prophetic calling usually implies Hittite (i.e.- terrorist) attacks throughout your life, so, cheer up. That battle with despair throughout your life is the result of a strong prophetic calling. God has a mighty calling for you; you have a strong prophetic purpose. Bear the brunt of the Hittite attack; be brave in Christ, and, with the passing of time, you will see the Hittite spirits fleeing from you in humiliating defeat, and your suffering and despair will serve as seed in the kingdom of God to produce mighty victories in the spirit realm that will bless and liberate the lives of many.

A person who suffers from deep emotional despair usually falls into states of **deep depression and sadness**. If you ever look into a person's eyes and perceive a sense of deep sadness and despair, you are looking into the eyes of a person under Hittite attack.

Since Hittite spirits prey on people's emotions, they like to stay in the dark and remain unseen to the mind, **whispering speculations** into the person's emotions. This means that people who have the nasty habit of spreading rumours and speculations are people who harbour Hittite spirits in their hearts.

Hittites are left-handed

In Judges chapter 3, the Word declares that the people of Israel did evil in the sight of God, and that God strengthened Eglon, the king of Moab, and sent him against the people of Israel, and he conquered them. After God's people repented, God raised up a man called Ehud to deliver His people:

"[14]*So the children of Israel served Eglon the king of Moab eighteen years. [15]But when the children of Israel cried unto the LORD, **the LORD raised them up a deliverer, Ehud the son of Gera**, a Benjamite, **a man lefthanded**: and by him the children of Israel sent a present unto Eglon the king of Moab. [16]But Ehud made him a dagger which had two edges, of a cubit length; and he did gird it under his raiment upon his right thigh.*

*17And he brought the present unto Eglon king of Moab: and Eglon was a very fat man. 18And when he had made an end to offer the present, he sent away the people that bare the present. 19But he himself turned again from the quarries that were by Gilgal, and said, **I have a secret errand unto thee**, O king: who said, Keep silence. And all that stood by him went out from him. 20And Ehud came unto him; and he was sitting in a summer parlour, which he had for himself alone. And Ehud said, I have a message from God unto thee. And he arose out of his seat. 21And Ehud put forth his left hand, and took the dagger from his right thigh, and thrust it into his belly: 22And the haft also went in after the blade; and the fat closed upon the blade, so that he could not draw the dagger out of his belly; and the dirt came out. 23Then Ehud went forth through the porch, and shut the doors of the parlour upon him, and locked them." (Judges 3:14-23)*

Notice how Ehud was able to kill Eglon (v21) because he was left-handed. Since most people are right-handed, Eglon was caught off-guard by Ehud's move with his left hand. This shows how, in Scripture, the left-hand side is related to things that are **unseen**, whilst the right-hand side is related to things that can be seen with the mind.

As many of you might already know, the right arm in the human body is controlled by the hemisphere in the brain that is in charge of logical reasoning, whilst the left arm is controlled by the hemisphere in the brain that is in charge of creative and intuitive processes. Logical, right-hand reasoning implies the knowledge of **truths** and the application of **laws** to combine these truths to form new laws and truths. Laws, by definition, set boundaries on what we can and cannot do, so they always imply **limitations**. Since limitations restrict our will, we can also say that abiding by laws implies the **death** of our will so that the will of another (in this case, the lawmaker) may be done. Laws are also **public** in nature; a law is useless if the lawmaker is the only one who knows it. Laws are also useless if there is no **authority** enforcing them, and as we shared in the previous chapter[11], Psalm 110 shows how the Lord associates the right-hand side with the establishment of authority. The right-hand side, therefore, is related to truth, laws, public openness, authority, structure, limitations, and death.

On the other hand (and I mean this literally), the left-hand side is related to creative and intuitive processes, so it implies **freedom**

---

[11] pg. 54

instead of limitations. In Scripture, freedom of access or movement is related to **grace**:

*"Let us therefore **come boldly unto the throne of grace**, that we may obtain mercy, and find grace to help in time of need."* (Hebrews 4:16)

*"[29]Conscience, I say, not thine own, but of the other: for **why is my liberty judged of another man's conscience?** [30]**For if I by grace be a partaker**, why am I evil spoken of for that for which I give thanks?" (1 Corinthians 10:29-30)*

Whilst Scripture links freedom to grace, grace itself is linked to **life**:

*"That as sin hath reigned unto death, even so might **grace reign** through righteousness **unto eternal life** by Jesus Christ our Lord."* (Romans 5:21)

*"Likewise, ye husbands, dwell with them according to knowledge, giving honour unto the wife, as unto the weaker vessel, and as being heirs together of the **grace of life**; that your prayers be not hindered."* (1 Peter 3:7)

In Scripture, freedom is also linked to the **spirit**:

*"Now the Lord is that Spirit: and where **the Spirit of the Lord** is, there is **liberty**."* (2 Corinthians 3:17)

When the Lord calls us to worship Him "in spirit and in truth" (John 4:24), He is calling us to worship Him with our left-hand side (spirit) and our right-hand side (truth).

The Lord also associates grace with intimacy:

*"[32]For the froward is abomination to the LORD: but his **secret** is with the righteous. [33]The curse of the LORD is in the house of the wicked: but he blesseth the habitation of the just. [34]Surely he scorneth the scorners: but he giveth **grace** unto the lowly."* (Proverbs 3:32-34)

Notice how verse 32 talks about God sharing "secrets", which speaks of intimacy, and how verse 34 ends by speaking of God giving **grace** to the humble. When the Lord invites us to "come boldly unto the **throne of grace**" in Hebrews 4:16, He is telling us that we have access to intimacy with Him. In ancient times, not anyone could approach the king:

*"All the king's servants, and the people of the king's provinces, do know, that whosoever, whether man or woman, shall come unto the king into the inner court, who is not called, there is one law of his to put him to death, except such to whom the king shall hold out the golden sceptre, that he may live: but **I have not been called to come in unto the king these thirty days**." (Esther 4:11)*

Only those who found grace in the eyes of the king could freely approach the throne:

*"²And it was so, when the king saw Esther the queen standing in the court, that **she obtained favour in his sight**: and the king held out to Esther the golden sceptre that was in his hand. So Esther drew near, and touched the top of the sceptre. ³Then said the king unto her, What wilt thou, queen Esther? and what is thy request? it shall be even given thee to the half of the kingdom."* (Esther 5:2-3)

The word translated as "favour" in verse 2 above is the Hebrew word *chen*, which is translated as "grace" in 38 other verses in the King James translation (I am still amazed by most translators' inconsistent translation of words from the original texts!) Therefore, verse 2 should really say, "She found **grace** in his sight". Once Esther found grace before the king, she was free to approach the throne, and the king asked her what the desires of her heart were (v3). This shows how grace opens the door for intimacy and for the sharing of secret intentions of the heart.

Besides being related to grace, freedom, life, and secrecy, the left-hand side is also related to **discovery**. Whilst the right-hand side is used to establish **known** truths, the left-hand side of creativity and intuition is used to explore and discover truths that are yet unknown.

Let us now compare the characteristics associated with each side:

Left-hand side	Right-hand side
Spirit	Truth
Grace	Law
Freedom	Limitations
Life	Death
"New", unknown truths	Established truths
Intuitive randomness	Structure
Unseen	Seen
Secrecy	Public openness
Hearing	Seeing

Scripture shows that our souls are made up of 3 components: the heart, the emotions, and the mind[12]. Often, Scripture refers to the emotions simply as "the soul", since the emotions are the most "notorious" component of the soul (this is equivalent to how the term "New York" can refer either to the American state of New York or to New York City, which is the "notorious" part of New York state). Considering the 3 components of the soul in light of what we have said so far, we can infer that the **mind** is on the right side of the soul whilst the **emotions** are on the left side. "Emotional" people (i.e.-people who give freedom to their emotions) tend to be more creative than those who are by nature logical thinkers. This is the reason why most singers, composers, painters, and poets are emotional people. The Lord placed emotions in our souls as a vital element for intuitive creation. Emotions can hear what the mind has yet to see. In conclusion, we can now make the following representation of the soul:

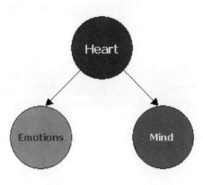

---

[12] You can read more on the 3 components of the soul (the mind, the emotions, and the heart) in the article "Male and female ministries", under the section "The role of pastors and teachers" (http://shamah-elim.info/mfmin.htm), and the article "3 levels of pastoring" (http://shamah-elim.info/3lvlpast.htm) posted on the Shamah-Elim Bible Studies website.

The heart is in the middle, since the heart is where the will resides (Ephesians 6:6), so it acts as the soul's **decision-maker**. It works with the mind and with the emotions to make decisions.

Since Hittite spirits are terrorists, they attack the emotions, and they always make an effort to go unseen by the mind. We can safely say, then, that Hittite spirits are "left-handed" spirits. This is confirmed by the following passage, which are words spoken by the Lord to Joshua as he entered the Promised Land:

"*³Every place that the sole of your foot shall tread upon, that have I given unto you, as I said unto Moses. ⁴From the wilderness and this Lebanon even unto the great river, the river Euphrates, **all the land of the Hittites**, and unto the great sea **toward the going down of the sun**, shall be your coast.*" (Joshua 1:3-4)

Notice that the Lord first refers to the "eastern" side of the Promised Land (the wilderness and "this Lebanon", all the way east to the Euphrates, in modern-day Iraq). Then he refers to the "western" side of the Promised Land (the land of the Hittites, all the way to the "Great Sea", i.e.- the Mediterranean Sea). When you look at a map where the north side is up, the **east** appears on the right-hand side, whilst the **west** is on the left-hand side. Since the Lord refers to the Hittites as being on the western side of the Promised Land, God is telling us that the Hittites are **left-handed spirits**. This apparently trivial fact is very important for the modern-day Joshuas who are called to take the spiritual Promised Land. It is interesting to note that, of all the peoples in the Promised Land (the Canaanites, the Jebusites, the Amorites, etc.), the Lord only mentions the "Hittites" by name when speaking to Joshua in the passage above. This is the reason why terrorist organisations such as Al-Qaeda (God curse them) are so prominent today. There is something happening in the spiritual atmosphere. The modern-day Joshuas are in spiritual anonymity, and the time is coming for them to take back the spiritual Promised Land. Since we are on the verge of a mighty spiritual revolution that will transform the spiritual atmosphere of the Earth, the Hittite spirits are currently very active. They fear for their "lives" because they know that the Joshua spirit is coming, so they are doing everything they can to prevent it being manifested.

God writes from right to left

Now that we know that the Hittites are left-handed, we must consider an important spiritual fact that will help us to defeat them. As most of you might already know, the Lord gave us this commandment:

"But seek ye first the kingdom of God, and his righteousness; and all these things shall be added unto you." (Matthew 6:33)

As we saw in the table above, the right-hand side is related to law, truth, and authority. Since laws are for the purpose of establishing **justice** (which, in Scripture, is usually translated as "righteousness"), we can infer from Matthew 6:33 above that God wants us to start on the "right" side (literally). When the intentions of our **hearts** and the thoughts of our **minds** are **selflessly** geared towards the execution of His will on Earth, not ours, then God Himself, not us, will move us towards the "left" side of grace; there, we will find grace before God and He will give us gifts, the greatest gift being the joy of being close to Him and knowing that we are considered beautiful (i.e.- full of grace) in His eyes.

Notice that, in Esther 5:2-3 quoted earlier[13], it is the king who authorises Esther to draw near by extending his golden sceptre and having Esther touch it. This is symbolic of Esther recognising his "kingship" over her life. Once she placed herself on the king's right-hand side, recognising his law and his authority, she could draw near and have access to his grace. In the same way, God wants us to place ourselves in the right-hand side first, in the side that implies truth, limitation, and death to our will. The right side is the "ugly" side, the "nasty" side, but it is the side we must place ourselves in so that we may enter into God's grace:

*"[14]**The secret of the LORD is with them that fear him**; and he will shew them his covenant. [15]Mine eyes are ever toward the LORD; for he shall pluck my feet out of the net. [16]Turn thee unto me, and **have mercy upon me**; for I am desolate and afflicted." (Psalm 25:14-16)*

> [The word translated as "mercy" in verse 16 is the Hebrew word *chanan*, which comes from the word *chen* meaning grace; therefore, verse 16 should really say "be **gracious** upon me"]

Notice that God shares His secrets with those who **fear Him**. Since the sharing of secrets is a sign of finding **grace** before God, Psalm 25

---

[13] pg. 63

above is saying that we find grace before Him when we have a heart that fears Him, a heart that is constantly concerned about His will and His spiritual laws, i.e.- a heart that **abides in truth**, on the right-hand side. You and I are beautiful in His eyes when our heart desires to abide in His will and judgements. We begin to look "ugly" when our hearts swerve from justice and judgement and start seeking our own selfish wills.

*"⁶But he giveth more grace. Wherefore he saith, God resisteth the proud, but **giveth grace unto the humble**. ⁷Submit yourselves therefore to God. Resist the devil, and he will flee from you." (James 4:6-8)*

Once again, finding grace before God is related to a humble heart that submits itself to His will. God wants us to start on the right-hand side, and He will automatically move us to the left-hand side. He calls us to **die** first so that He may **resurrect** us to life in Him; death comes before resurrection. God gives you natural life so that you may give it back as a seed in order to reap eternal life in Him. This spiritual process takes place during a believer's entire life, and is stymied only when the believer decides to hoggishly cling to his or her natural life and to live as if there was no spiritual inheritance[14] to fight for.

Truth produces death to our self-will, but death, ironically, produces freedom. For example, people who have died literally and have come back to tell the story speak of how their souls were able to freely move about and how they were able to see events that were happening many miles away. The "advent of freedom upon death" is certified by the following passages:

*"²For the woman which hath an husband is bound by the law to her husband so long as he liveth; but if the husband be dead, she is loosed from the law of her husband. ³So then if, while her husband liveth, she be married to another man, she shall be called an adulteress: but **if her husband be dead, she is free from that law**; so that she is no adulteress, though she be married to another man." (Romans 7:2-3)*

*"For he that is **dead is freed** from sin." (Romans 6:7)*

---

[14] You can read more on the spiritual inheritance God has for us in the article titled "What is your inheritance?" posted on the Shamah-Elim Bible Studies website (http://shamah-elim.info/inherit.htm).

Since truth produces death, and this death produces freedom, the Lord declares that the final result of truth is freedom:

"*31Then said Jesus to those Jews which believed on him, If ye continue in my word, then are ye my disciples indeed; 32And **ye shall know the truth, and the truth shall make you free**." (John 8:31-32)*

What most preachers refuse to understand about this passage is that truth produces freedom **through death of self**. This is the reason why John 8:32 is split into two parts: "knowing the truth" and "the truth making us free". When we start on the right side, the side of truth, God will take us to the left side, the side of freedom and resurrection life.

As most of you may know, the Hebrew language is written from right to left, as opposed to most Western languages, in which words are written from left to right. The spiritual reason why God made the Jewish people write from right to left is because the right-hand side must come first. When the sun comes up every morning, it appears in the east, which is the right side, and it makes its voyage across the heavens to disappear in the west, which is the left side. God writes things from right to left. It is carnal man who has turned the Gospel into a left-handed affair, emphasising grace, liberty, life, and all the "goodies" whilst downplaying the Word of justice and judgement, the Word of Truth and Righteousness that God wants us to preach first. When the Church finally understands that things must start on the right side, the greatest flow of "left-handed" grace and power in human history will begin to be manifested. The **river of God** starts on the right side and flows to the left:

*"Afterward he brought me again unto the door of the house; and, behold, **waters issued out from under the threshold of the house eastward**: for the forefront of the house stood toward the east, and the waters came down from under from the right side of the house, at the south side of the altar." (Ezekiel 47:1)*
> [The word "eastward" here is referring to the threshold, not to the flow of the waters; in other words, the waters were issuing from the threshold that looked towards the east, as the rest of the verse explains]

A left-handed "gospel" draws the Hittites

When pastors preach a "gospel" that tries to sidestep the "not so gracious" right-hand side, they automatically draw in the Hittites. Many pastors seem to believe that the New Testament God is a God of "kindness and blessings", a God with whom everything is "good and happy", a God with whom believers don't have to die or suffer in the slightest bit. Any type of inconvenient suffering and heartache is automatically labelled as "satan's work", and is immediately "rebuked". **The Gospel has unfortunately been distorted by man into a "gospel" in which we study the Bible to see what we can get from God, not to know what God is requiring of us.** When the right-hand side (which deals with truth, law, judgement, justice, and death) is ignored, the mind of the believer is weakened and the only thing that is being "fed" is the believer's **emotions**, which lie on the left side of his or her soul. Emotions are not bad in and of themselves; in fact, they are **very important** to unleash God's **prophetic power**. But, when they are unrestrained by a *"right" mind* focused on God's judgements and justice and by a *"right" heart* that seeks to be submitted under God's will, **emotions** are prone to hearing and being stirred by Hittite spirits of deceit.

A study of passages such as Jeremiah 20 and Habakkuk 3 reveal that the most "**emotional**" of all the ministries is the prophetic ministry. This is the reason why the prophetic ministry is the one most linked with music in Scripture (2 Kings 3:15, 1 Samuel 10:15), since music is a powerful evoker of emotions. This is also why the people who seemed to do the **craziest** things in Scripture always seemed to be prophets (if you don't believe this, I strongly invite you to read these chapters, to get a *taste* of how wild and crazy prophets can be: Isaiah 20, Ezekiel 4, Ezekiel 5, and Jeremiah 13). A person goes "crazy" when his emotions override his natural mind, and prophets are called by God to allow God's emotions to flow through them, overriding any inhibitions set by the natural mind. This is why the speaking of tongues was the first thing believers did when receiving the baptism of the Holy Spirit (Acts 2:1-4), since speaking in tongues implies saying things that your natural mind cannot comprehend. The baptism of the Holy Spirit, i.e.- being enveloped in the Holy Spirit, is constantly related in Scripture to the **prophetic anointing** (Joel 2:28) because the Holy Spirit is prophetic in nature. Prophets are called to do and say things that they may not fully understand with their natural minds, and that is the reason why they sometimes seem to be crazy "drunkards" who have "lost their mind" (Acts 2:12-13, 1 Samuel 1:14-20).

Having said all of the above, we must also say that, if a prophet is not restrained by a **mind** bound by God's judgements and a **heart** submissive to God's will, he or she is prone to having his or her **emotions** taken over by left-handed Hittite spirits that take advantage of those emotions and use them to drive them into purposelessness. In 2 Chronicles chapter 18, the Holy Spirit shows us how a group of prophets were prophesying before kings Ahab and Jehoshaphat, saying that God would grant them victory against the Syrians. Ahab, who was an evil king, believed in "consulting the Lord" only when he could expect to hear a "good report", ignoring God's word when it went against his carnal desires; in other words, Ahab, king of the northern kingdom of Israel, was "**left**-based", a believer in "***truthless grace***". Jehoshaphat, on the other hand, was a righteous king who sometimes committed the sin of "hanging out with the wrong crowd". Since Jehoshaphat, king of the southern kingdom of Judah, believed in a "**right**-based", "***truth-first***" relationship with God, he was able to discern a spirit of error in these prophets, and asked Ahab if he had some other prophet who could confirm or refute this "word of victory". The Bible then records the following:

"*⁷And the king of Israel said unto Jehoshaphat, There is yet one man, by whom we may enquire of the LORD: but **I hate him; for he never prophesied good unto me, but always evil**: the same is Micaiah the son of Imla. And Jehoshaphat said, Let not the king say so. ⁸And the king of Israel called for one of his officers, and said, Fetch quickly Micaiah the son of Imla. ⁹And the king of Israel and Jehoshaphat king of Judah sat either of them on his throne, clothed in their robes, and they sat in a void place at the entering in of the gate of Samaria; and all the prophets prophesied before them.*" (2 Chronicles 18:7-9)

Ahab hated Micaiah, because Micaiah always told him the truth; in other words, Micaiah always prophesied (a left-handed act) whilst abiding in truth (a right-handed base). The other prophets were more interested in submitting to the will of human authority, i.e.- king Ahab, than to the will of God, so they always ended up prophesying the king's will. As you continue to read, it becomes obvious that the "**false prophets**" were **real** prophets. They really did have a prophetic calling on their lives. What made them "*false*" was not the fact that they were not prophets, but the fact that they did not abide in truth, and anyone who ignores the truth automatically enters into falsehood, since whatever is not true is false by definition. A "false" U.S. dollar bill, for example, is a real bill; it is not imaginary. What makes it false is that it claims to be printed by the U.S. Federal government when, in fact, it was probably printed on a modern colour printer in someone's home.

A false prophet, therefore, might give a false prophecy and actually "feel" a strong spiritual presence as he or she gives the prophecy. He or she might utter words that are not coming from his or her mind but are actually being given to the prophet by a spirit moving through his or her emotions (as is always the case when one prophesies). In the case of the prophets of 2 Chronicles 18, the spiritual presence they felt was not God's presence, but, rather, a spirit of deceit sent by God Himself to deceive Ahab and the prophets, as Micaiah declared when he was brought before the kings:

"*18Again he said, Therefore hear the word of the LORD; I saw the LORD sitting upon his throne, and all the host of heaven standing on his right hand and on his left. 19And the LORD said, Who shall entice Ahab king of Israel, that he may go up and fall at Ramothgilead? And one spake saying after this manner, and another saying after that manner. 20Then there came out a spirit, and stood before the LORD, and said, I will entice him. And the LORD said unto him, Wherewith? 21And he said, **I will go out, and be a lying spirit in the mouth of all his prophets. And the LORD said, Thou shalt entice him, and thou shalt also prevail: go out, and do even so**. 22Now therefore, behold, the LORD hath put a lying spirit in the mouth of these thy prophets, and the LORD hath spoken evil against thee. 23Then Zedekiah the son of Chenaanah came near, and smote Micaiah upon the cheek, and said, Which way went the Spirit of the LORD from me to speak unto thee? 24And Micaiah said, Behold, thou shalt see on that day when thou shalt go into an inner chamber to hide thyself. 25Then the king of Israel said, Take ye Micaiah, and carry him back to Amon the governor of the city, and to Joash the king's son; 26And say, Thus saith the king, Put this fellow in the prison, and feed him with bread of affliction and with water of affliction, until I return in peace. 27And Micaiah said, If thou certainly return in peace, then hath not the LORD spoken by me. And he said, Hearken, all ye people.*" (2 Chronicles 18:18-27)*

Micaiah preferred to give a true prophetic word and go to prison rather than yield to the atmosphere of deceit that surrounded him at the moment (Revelation 2:8-11). Micaiah was a prophet whose emotions were used by God to give prophetic word because his heart and his mind abided in the not-so-pleasant-and-comfortable side: the right side.

Notice how Zedekiah slapped Micaiah and asked him, "When did the Spirit of the LORD go from me to you?" (v23). This means that Zedekiah, who had a legitimate prophetic calling, actually felt some type of spiritual presence flowing through him as he prophesied, and he thought that this presence was God. Those of you who have given a prophetic word know that, sometimes, you get goose bumps and feel a strong presence running through your physical being as you prophesy, and this is what Zedekiah felt. This physical sensation is not unusual when giving prophecy, since, as we said above, prophetic word is given when a spirit (hopefully God's!) is flowing through your emotions, overriding your natural understanding:

"For we know in part, and we prophesy in part." (1 Corinthians 13:9)

However, if your heart is not **right**, and if you constantly avoid the pain of abiding in His truth and living under His constant judgements, God Himself will allow you to be exposed to a spirit of deceit that will "feel" just like God's Spirit. When God sees you placing your faith in your emotions and not in His truth (that kills self-will), He will make sure that those emotions deceive you (2 Thessalonians 2:9-11). Don't idolise your emotions!! Don't put the left side before the right side. It's like putting the cart before the horse.

Some of you may be asking, "How can we **know** that the spirit of deceit that was in the prophets of 2 Chronicles 18 was a **Hittite** spirit?" A combination of facts provides the evidence:

❑   First, the fact that Hittites attack the emotions, and the false prophets felt strong emotions flowing through them

❑   Second, the fact that Hittites, like any "good" terrorist, **disguise themselves**, pretending to be friends when they are really foes. In 2 Chronicles 18:29, when Ahab and Jehoshaphat decided to fight against the Syrians (ignoring Micaiah's word), Ahab told Jehoshaphat to wear kingly robes, even when Ahab himself had already chosen to wear a disguise for the battle. Jehoshaphat's obedience to this request almost cost him his life (2 Chronicles 18:30-32). The fact that Ahab decided to disguise himself and used Jehoshaphat as bait for the Syrian army is a "classical" Hittite move.

❑   Third, the death of Ahab in verse 32 was caused by an arrow shot at random. The arrow is different from the sword because an arrow does not require you to be close to your enemy in order to kill him. The arrow allows you to hide in a dark place and kill your enemy from a distance, in much the same way that a modern-day sniper can. Those of you who live in the U.S. surely remember the "D.C. sniper" who caused **terror** in 2003 by randomly killing people in the Washington, D.C. area. Ahab's death by a random arrow is God's prophetic way of telling us that Ahab died because he allowed Hittite spirits of terror into his heart. This "random" arrow was shot in the spirit realm by Micaiah when he gave prophetic word in **truth**.

It is worth noting that, just as the Hittites can shoot arrows from the dark, their spiritual "parallels" in the realm of righteousness --- God's **prophetic** people --- can shoot prophetic word into the atmosphere and impact distant places. My brother and sister in Christ, you are called to move in the prophetic anointing (Revelation 19:10, Psalm 105:15). Engage in spiritual warfare against principalities and powers. Shoot prophetic word into the atmosphere in prayer, and rest assured that those arrows will impact places near and far, and you will be paving the way for God's glory to be manifested on Earth. No one might see you as you shoot your arrows from your prayer closet. You will probably not get any human recognition, but the One who sees the things that are hidden will reward you in public (Matthew 6:5-6), and, believe you me, the greatest reward is to see our Father's will fulfilled on Earth (Matthew 6:9-10). When you are dead to self, His desires become your desires, and His victories become your victories. As you continue to do this, you prepare yourself to be made One with Him for eternity -- this is the **true** eternal **life**.

When the Lord said the following through the prophet Hosea, He was referring to today's Church:

"*¹⁴And they have not cried unto me with their heart, when they howled upon their beds: they assemble themselves for corn and wine, and they rebel against me. ¹⁵Though I have bound and strengthened their arms, yet do they imagine mischief against me. ¹⁶**They return, but not to the most High: they are like a deceitful bow**: their princes shall fall by the sword for the rage of their tongue: this shall be their derision in the land of Egypt.*" (Hosea 7:14-16)

Hittite roach-killer

Since Hittites can only thrive wherever the "right side" is ignored, they are automatically driven away when the right side is restored. Hittites are spirits of chaos and disorder, and they hate the establishment of law and justice. This is why the Al Qaeda Hittites (God curse them) and other terrorists are making such a concerted effort to cause chaos in Iraq and to prevent the establishment of a

just government there. It was **God's prophetic purpose** (not George W. Bush's) for Saddam Hussein to be toppled in Iraq. Hussein's fall acts as a prophetic seed that will unleash the fall of countless spiritual Amorites in the years to come. The fall of Iraq is a prophetic figure of the fall of Babylon (Revelation 17 and 18), which represents the fall of the pastoral matriarchy[15] in the Church. This is why the war in Iraq has stirred up so much emotion. It is amazing how people around the world who would move heaven and earth to save a stranded whale protested so fiercely to preserve the regime of a savage man who ruthlessly murdered thousands of his own people. God bless the men and women who have sacrificially given of themselves to liberate Iraq. Their sacrifice is unleashing powerful spiritual consequences that will bless millions and millions of people in the years ahead. Despite George W. Bush's initial hesitation, Tony Blair's **UN**-helpful **interference**, and a world of Canaanite protestors, Saddam Hussein the Amorite was toppled, and many more Amorites (spiritual and literal) will be toppled in the years to come. Hallelujah!!! (Revelation 19:1-3)

In Proverbs, the Lord declares the following:

*"Where there is no vision, the people perish: but **he that keepeth the law**, happy is he." (Proverbs 29:18)*

God provides the Church with **vision** through the **prophetic anointing**. When Hittites enter a place, they pervert the prophetic anointing, as we saw in 2 Chronicles 18. This means that, upon their entry, Hittites rob people of true prophetic vision, and, according to Proverbs 29:18 above, this causes the perishing of the people, which refers to the wasting away of the believers' gifts, ministries, and God's wonderful prophetic calling for their lives. Notice, however, that Proverbs 29:18 ends by referring to the "law". This means that the venom that kills vision-robbing Hittite spirits is God's law, i.e. - the "right" side.

As the "right side" is re-established and the **word of justice and judgement** is restored in the Church, the Hittite spirits of purposelessness will be driven away. This is the Hittite roach killer.

---

[15] You can read more on the "pastoral matriarchy" in the prophetic word titled "Bread in the sea" posted on the Shamah-Elim Bible Studies website (http://shamah-elim.info/p_breadsea.htm).

"Public" grace draws the Hittites

Before ending this chapter, an important issue must be addressed concerning the Hittites. As we mentioned on pg. 64, the Hittites are left-handed spirits, and the "left-hand side" is associated in Scripture with things such as grace; the word "grace" is related to the concept of beauty and elegance, so the word "grace" could very easily be replaced by the word "beauty". We also saw, however, that the left-hand side is also related to "secrecy". This means that, in a "strange" sort of way, "beauty" and "secrecy" are intimately linked. How?

Physical beauty is a God-given gift. It is not the devil's invention. The underlying **truth** behind the grace of your physical beauty is that it was fundamentally designed to draw people to God's beauty, not to you, in the same way that the burning bush served to draw the attention of Moses to God's word for him, not to the burning bush itself. When you read the story of the burning bush in Exodus chapters 3 and 4, you will notice that Moses was drawn to "behold this great sight" of a bush that would not be consumed by the fire, in the same way that any of us might feel compelled to stare at a beautiful sunset, or in the same way that a young man might feel compelled to stare at a beautiful young lady. In the early verses of Exodus 3, the word "bush" is mentioned **5** times (which is a figure of the fivefold ministry of Ephesians 4:11 and represents "**grace to minister**"), and is not mentioned again in the rest of the passage. In fact, the Hebrew word cenah that is translated as "bush" in Exodus 3, only appears again in Deuteronomy 33:16, never to appear again in the Bible. This means that, after Exodus 3:4, Moses' focus was not on the bush but on the **One** who was speaking from the bush. If you are a pretty young lady, you might draw the stares of young men when you are out in the street walking, but, if you are in the Spirit, those few seconds of "stare time" will serve as a spiritual point of contact for that young man to experience God's holy presence, in the same way that Moses did when he approached the bush; remember that the first thing that God told Moses was to not get any closer and to take off his sandals because he was standing on holy ground. Young sister in Christ, if God gave you physical beauty, consecrate that beauty unto Him and allow that beauty to serve as a means to draw people's attention to the Almighty and Holy God that abides in you. Don't use that physical grace to be admired and worshipped by men. That would be self-glorification. Using your physical grace to promote "**you**" would mean separating that grace from the **truth** foundation that justifies that grace, and a grace not founded on truth becomes, by definition, a "**false** grace", since the opposite of truth is falsehood.

Even if you consecrate your physical beauty unto God, you must also understand that there is only so much grace you may exhibit in public. In Exodus 3:5, God tells Moses not to draw any closer to the bush. God did not expose anymore of Himself to Moses until Moses **committed** to God's calling for his life. In the same way, there are certain dimensions of your physical beauty that **must not** be exposed in public. The **deep** enjoyment of another person's grace can only be done in intimacy that is covered by a **commitment**, i.e.- a covenant. For example, you cannot truly enjoy another person's friendship until that friendship reaches a level of trust at which you can tell each other secrets, and share your deepest hopes and fears. Exposing yourself like that to a stranger who has not entered into a true friendship covenant with you would be **suicide**. Spouses can enjoy each other's physical beauty in a deep way because they know that the other person has made a commitment to share the rest of their lives with them, vowing to have such intimacy with no one but the other spouse. Doing this outside of a covenant is, again, an act of **suicide**. You can't throw your "holy things" (i.e.- your inner treasures) to the dogs, because they will trample on them and then try to destroy you (Matthew 7:6).

As you can see, grace (i.e.- beauty) and secrecy (or intimacy) are deeply intertwined. When you expose deep and intimate levels of grace or beauty in public, you are removing the truth foundation of your beauty, since **true beauty** can only reign in a righteous environment:

*"That as sin hath reigned unto death, even so might **grace reign through righteousness** unto eternal life by Jesus Christ our Lord." (Romans 5:21)*

The exposing of intimate beauty, when abiding **in truth**, demands a "death covenant" on the part of the person who will enjoy that beauty. The marriage covenant, for example, is a "death sentence" to your will. By marrying the other person, you are saying, "I am giving my natural life to you, and I will not have deep, deep intimacy with any other person on the face of the Earth but you". When such a "death covenant" is not demanded, the exposing of intimate beauty loses its truth foundation and becomes false beauty, i.e.- left-handed beauty with no right-hand side, and, as we saw before, this opens the way for Hittite spirits of purposelessness to enter. This is why men and women who improperly expose themselves physically to other people end up having constant bouts with depression, despair, and sometimes even suicide. This is why prostitutes usually become drug addicts in their quest to flee from the torment of the Hittite spirits that they have drawn upon themselves by their constant exposition of intimate beauty without demanding a "covenant in truth". This is also why many congregations have lost their **true** prophetic anointing, because young "sisters" go around the congregation wearing low-rise trousers and other provocative clothes, exposing their physical grace in public, and thereby drawing Hittite spirits that slowly suck up the true prophetic anointing in their own lives and in the lives of those in the congregation.

So much more to say

There is so much more left to say about the Hittite spirits!! For example, there is an intricate relationship between the Hittite spirits and Sheol (i.e.- hell); Hittite spirits can actually be called "spirits from Sheol".

"*⁵The **sorrows of hell compassed me** about: the snares of death prevented me. ⁶In my distress I called upon the LORD, and cried unto my God: he heard my voice out of his temple, and my cry came before him, even into his ears. ⁷Then the earth shook and trembled; the foundations also of the hills moved and were shaken, because he was wroth. ⁸There went up a smoke out of his nostrils, and fire out of his mouth devoured: coals were kindled by it. ⁹He bowed the heavens also, and came down: and darkness was under his feet. ¹⁰And he rode upon a cherub, and did fly: yea, he did fly upon the wings of the wind. ¹¹He made darkness his secret place; his pavilion round about him were dark waters and thick clouds of the skies. ¹²At the brightness that was before him his thick clouds passed, hail stones and coals of fire. ¹³The LORD also thundered in the heavens, and the Highest gave his voice; hail stones and coals of fire. ¹⁴Yea, **he sent out his arrows**, and scattered them; and he shot out lightnings, and discomfited them. ¹⁵Then the channels of waters were seen, and the foundations of the world were discovered at thy rebuke, O LORD, at the blast of the breath of thy nostrils. ¹⁶He sent from above, he took me, he drew me out of many waters. ¹⁷He delivered me from my strong enemy, and from them which hated me: for they were too strong for me. ¹⁸They prevented me in the day of my calamity: but the LORD was my stay. ¹⁹He brought me forth also into a large place; he delivered me, because he delighted in me.*" (Psalm 18:5-18)

To learn more about Hittite spirits, we recommend the following postings from the Shamah-Elim Bible Studies website:

- Article "The stinging mustard seed"
  (http://shamah-elim.info/mustard.htm)
- Article "Jonah's journey"
  (http://shamah-elim.info/jonahjrn.htm)
- Article "Pre-parousia – The green horse"
  (http://shamah-elim.info/preparu5.htm)
- Prophetic word "The 8 terrorists"
  (http://shamah-elim.info/p_terror8.htm)
- Prophetic word "Floods in Eastern Europe", section "Hittite Eastern Europe"
  (http://shamah-elim.info/p_floodeu.htm#Hittite_Eastern_Europe)

Chapter 5
The Canaanites

This chapter will focus on the "Canaanites". Just like the Hittites, the Canaanites target people's emotions. However, the Canaanites' mode of attack focuses mostly on modifying people's thinking patterns, striving to get people to judge based on "warm" emotions rather than on the sometimes "cold" truth. Whilst Hittites turn people into proactive fighters for lost causes, Canaanites turn people into active seekers of "communal pleasure" and false "bliss".

An article similar to this chapter is posted on the Shamah-Elim Bible Studies website at the following web address:
http://shamah-elim.info/cananite.htm

What's in a name?

A great deal can be inferred directly from the meaning of the word "Canaanite", which means, "lowlands people". Since the word "land" is related to the concept of "earth" or "ground", the "lowlands" refer to **low earthly passions**. Canaanite spirits are the spirits behind **addictions and sexual perversions**. This is why Sodom and Gomorrah are portrayed in Scriptures as Canaanite cities:

*"19And the border of the **Canaanites** was from Sidon, as thou comest to Gerar, unto Gaza; as thou goest, unto **Sodom, and Gomorrah**, and Admah, and Zeboim, even unto Lasha."* (Genesis 10:19)

*"12Abram dwelled in the **land of Canaan**, and Lot dwelled in the cities of the plain, and pitched his tent toward **Sodom**. 13But the men of Sodom were wicked and sinners before the LORD exceedingly"* (Genesis 13:12-13)

The spirits of homosexuality and lesbianism, along with all other sexual perversions, are Canaanite spirits. These spirits operate through people's **emotions** and make a concerted effort to **shut off the person's mind**, since the mind is the part of the soul most related to making **judgements**; the conscience resides in the mind, and the mind is the one designed to store God's laws and apply them with wisdom to make judgements:

*"¹³Which things also we speak, not in the words which man's wisdom teacheth, but which the Holy Ghost teacheth; comparing spiritual things with spiritual. ¹⁴But the natural man receiveth not the things of the Spirit of God: for they are foolishness unto him: neither can he know them, because they are spiritually discerned. ¹⁵But **he that is spiritual judgeth all things**, yet he himself is judged of no man. ¹⁶For who hath known **the mind of the Lord**, that he may instruct him? But we have the mind of Christ." (1 Corinthians 2:13-16)*

*"¹⁵Which shew the work of the law written in their hearts, their **conscience** also bearing witness, and their thoughts the mean while accusing or else excusing one another;) ¹⁶In the day when **God shall judge** the secrets of men by Jesus Christ according to my gospel." (Romans 2:15-16)*

People who fall into alcoholism (which is a Canaanite spirit) generally start drinking through someone or something convincing them that heavy drinking is "normal" and is being "done by everyone". Once the person's judgement against heavy drinking has been "shut off", the person starts drinking, and, soon, the alcohol shuts off all sober judgement and inhibition; that is when the person goes into a strong and public display of emotions. Canaanite spirits are **spirits of carnal excess and dissolution**:

*"¹⁵See then that ye walk circumspectly, not as fools, but as **wise**, ¹⁶Redeeming the time, because the days are evil. ¹⁷Wherefore be ye not unwise, but understanding what the will of the Lord is. ¹⁸And **be not drunk with wine**, wherein is excess; but be filled with the Spirit" (Ephesians 5:15-18)*

As we saw on pg. 64, the **mind** is right-handed and *truth-oriented*, whilst the **emotions** are left-handed and *grace-oriented*. Canaanite spirits, therefore, are left-handed spirits that emphasise freedom and grace, downplaying truth and judgement, just as Hittite spirits do. In the previous chapter, we saw that Hittites are distorters of prophetic emotions; they drive people to suicide and despair by portraying a prophetic vision that is not truth-based; Hittites are the spirits that drive terrorists to commit suicide attacks and to shed their lives for **false** causes; wherever Hittites invade, a sense of chaos, purposelessness, and **emptiness** soon sets in. If the Hittites are distorters of **prophetic** emotions, what type of emotions do the Canaanites distort? It is important to know the answer to this question in order to prevent these types of spirits entering our lives, and to drive them out if they already entered. We will address this question in the next few sections.

Canaanites are "dancers"

In Genesis 13, the Lord records the separation of Abraham from Lot and Lot's decision to live in the Canaanite city of Sodom:

"^{10}And Lot lifted up his eyes, and beheld all **the plain** of Jordan, that it was well watered every where, before the LORD destroyed **Sodom and Gomorrah**, even as the garden of the LORD, like the land of Egypt, as thou comest unto Zoar. ^{11}Then Lot chose him all the plain of Jordan; and Lot journeyed east: and they separated themselves the one from the other. ^{12}Abram dwelled in **the land of Canaan**, and Lot dwelled in the cities of the plain, and pitched his tent toward Sodom. ^{13}But the men of Sodom were wicked and sinners before the LORD exceedingly." (Genesis 13:10-13)

The word "plain" that appears in this passage is translated from the Hebrew word *kikkar*, which comes from the Hebrew word *karar*; oddly enough, *karar* means, "to whirl, to dance". Therefore, the phrase "cities of the plain" in verse 12 could, in a way, be paraphrased as "cities of dancing". The reason why the Lord decided to connect the word "plain" with the seemingly unrelated word "dancing" in the Hebrew language is to illustrate the connexion between Canaanite spirits and "dancing". Please, don't misunderstand me. **Dancing is not wrong in and of itself**. In fact, it is sometimes the **right** thing to do. However, "dancing" that is not led by the Spirit of God is directly associated with Canaanite spirits. When the Bible refers to "dancing", it refers to more than the act of "shaking your *bad* self", as we will see later in this chapter.

As you all know from the movie (or from reading the Bible), the people of Israel rebelled against God whilst Moses was up on Mount Sinai receiving God's commandments for His people. They built a golden calf, called it "God", and decided to throw a party and celebrate:

"^{5}And when Aaron saw it, he built an altar before it; and Aaron made proclamation, and said, To morrow is a feast to the LORD. ^{6}And they rose up early on the morrow, and offered burnt offerings, and brought peace offerings; and the people sat down to eat and to drink, and rose up to play." (Exodus 32:5-6)

When Moses came down from the mount, this is what the Word declares:

*"¹⁹And it came to pass, as soon as he came nigh unto the camp, that he saw the calf, and the **dancing**: and Moses' anger waxed hot, and he cast the tables out of his hands, and brake them beneath the mount. ²⁰And he took the calf which they had made, and burnt it in the fire, and ground it to powder, and strawed it upon the water, and made the children of Israel drink of it." (Exodus 32:19-20)*

Notice how this passage relates "dancing" in the flesh with carnal excess and dissolution, emphasising the relationship between "dancing" and Canaanite spirits.

Mad cow disease

The passage quoted above (Exodus 32:19-20) also establishes a connexion between "calves" and "dancing". The word translated as "calf" in this passage is the Hebrew word *egel*, which comes from another Hebrew word meaning, "to revolve". In a sense, we can say that the children of Israel were revolving around the calf, i.e.- dancing around the calf, in the same way that a woman would sensually dance around a man she likes. Since the word *egel* for "calf" in Hebrew has a "masculine" connotation, we can say that the calf was a "young bull", meaning that the children of Israel were like "female cattle", or "cows", dancing around the young bull. A close study of passages such as 1 Samuel 6 reveals that there is a strong connexion between "cows" and Canaanite spirits. This connexion is the spiritual reason behind the outbreaks of "mad cow disease" in recent years. As you may have seen on television, cows with this disease can't walk straight and look very much like "drunken cows". From what I have heard on educational channels, the organisms that cause this disease take residence in the cow's brain, making any meat that has been in contact with cow brains very dangerous. As we said above, Canaanite spirits make a concerted effort to shut down the person's **mind** and to get him or her into a drunken stupor in which emotions are no longer inhibited by a sober mind. This is the spiritual reason why the "mad cow" organisms attack the **brain**, of all places. God has allowed the manifestation of this disease in these latter days to portray the current condition of His Church, which has allowed herself to be under a pastoral shield[16] that emphasises a gospel of "grace" and

---

[16] You can read more on the unrighteous "pastoral shield" in the article titled "Can a believer be sick for the sake of others?", under the section "The pastoral

blessing and downplays God's justice and judgements. We are like the children of Israel in Exodus 32 who have fashioned a calf, a "God" according to our own likings and soulish interests, and we dance around this "God" as if we were holding a sacred feast for the One True God (Exodus 32:5). We even bring our "burnt offerings" and "peace offerings" (Exodus 32:6) before this "God", pretending to be right with God and pretending that we are doing all that God requires of us. God, however, sees His Church as a herd of mad cows, drunk on the spiritual gifts that He Himself gave to them, in the same way that the people of Israel feasted using the very provisions that God had given to them through the Egyptians when they left Egypt:

"[35]And the children of Israel did according to the word of Moses; and **they borrowed of the Egyptians jewels of silver**, and jewels of gold, and raiment: [36]And the LORD gave the people favour in the sight of the Egyptians, so that they lent unto them such things as they required. And they spoiled the Egyptians." (Exodus 12:35-36)

This is the end-time and God's prophetic Word shall be fulfilled. He will lift up a mighty prophetic Church in the latter days that will shake the spiritual foundations of this Earth and manifest God's latter-rain glory. As this spiritual Church is raised up, God's judgements will become more and more evident throughout the Earth. In the last chapter of the Old Testament, the Lord's manifestation is equated with the rising of the "sun of righteousness" (or the "sun of justice", as I prefer to translate it):

"[1]For, behold, the day cometh, that shall burn as an oven; and all the proud, yea, and all that do wickedly, shall be stubble: and the **day that cometh shall burn them up**, saith the LORD of hosts, that it shall leave them neither root nor branch. [2]But unto you that fear my name shall the **Sun of righteousness arise** with healing in his wings; and ye shall go forth, and grow up as **calves of the stall**. [3]And **ye shall tread down the wicked**; for they shall be ashes under the soles of your feet in the day that I shall do this, saith the LORD of hosts. [4]Remember ye the law of Moses my servant, which I commanded unto him in Horeb for all Israel, with the statutes and judgments. [5]Behold, I will send you Elijah the prophet before the coming of the great and dreadful day of the LORD: [6]And he shall turn the heart of the fathers to

---

shield", posted on the Shamah-Elim Bible Studies website (http://shamah-elim.info/sickothr.htm).

the children, and the heart of the children to their fathers, lest I come and smite the earth with a curse." (Malachi 4:1-6)

Notice that God's latter-day manifestation is not equated with rainbows, smiley faces, and a field of beautiful roses with delicate butterflies dancing all around. Our God is a holy God, and when He manifests Himself, the weight of His Glory and Righteousness is strong!!!

*"For our light affliction, which is but for a moment, worketh for us a far more exceeding and **eternal weight of glory**" (2 Corinthians 4:17)*

*"[17]And if children, then heirs; heirs of God, and joint-heirs with Christ; if so be that we suffer with him, that we may be also glorified together. [18]For I reckon that **the sufferings of this present time are not worthy to be compared with the glory which shall be revealed in us**. [19]For the earnest expectation of the creature waiteth for the manifestation of the sons of God." (Romans 8:17-19)*

As Malachi 4:6 declares, the spirit of Elijah is to return, and as it does, God's judgements will be made increasingly manifested on Earth, and it will be through God's prophetic remnant people that these judgements will be released on Earth. Mad cow disease is a physical manifestation of a judgement that God is beginning to carry out in the spirit world against the Canaanite spirits. You and I, my brother and sister, are agents of God's spiritual judgements on Earth. Whilst Canaanite pastors, the **modern-day Aarons**, are fashioning the "gospel" to the liking of the world and the flesh, God's remnant Church is living a life of submission to God, abiding under God's constant judgements, **being moulded by God instead of them trying to mould God to their own liking**.

Dancers are pleasers

Now that we have found a spiritual connexion between dancing and Canaanites, we must understand the spiritual meaning of dancing. In Mark chapter 6, the Holy Spirit records the following "dancing incident":

"[17]For Herod himself had sent forth and laid hold upon John, and bound him in prison for Herodias' sake, his brother Philip's wife: for he had married her. [18]For John had said unto Herod, It is not lawful for thee to have thy brother's wife. [19]Therefore Herodias

had a quarrel against him, and would have killed him; but she could not: ²⁰For Herod feared John, knowing that he was a just man and an holy, and observed him; and when he heard him, he did many things, and heard him gladly. ²¹And when a convenient day was come, that Herod on his birthday made a supper to his lords, high captains, and chief estates of Galilee; ²²And **when the daughter of the said Herodias came in, and danced, and pleased Herod** and them that sat with him, the king said unto the damsel, Ask of me whatsoever thou wilt, and I will give it thee. ²³And he sware unto her, Whatsoever thou shalt ask of me, I will give it thee, unto the half of my kingdom. ²⁴And she went forth, and said unto her mother, What shall I ask? And she said, The head of John the Baptist. ²⁵And she came in straightway with haste unto the king, and asked, saying, I will that thou give me by and by in a charger the head of John the Baptist. ²⁶And **the king was exceeding sorry; yet for his oath's sake, and for their sakes which sat with him, he would not reject her.** ²⁷And immediately the king sent an executioner, and commanded his head to be brought: and he went and beheaded him in the prison, ²⁸And brought his head in a charger, and gave it to the damsel: and the damsel gave it to her mother." (Mark 6:17-28)

Notice that verse 22 above says that Herodias' daughter danced and **pleased** Herod. Dancing is, in essence, an act of pleasing others. This is why they have dancers in strip clubs; these dancers, who are women trapped by Canaanite spirits, dance around the client, doing all the moves that the client may find "pleasant". Women who are good tango dancers are those who are very good at following the lead of their male partner, which is, in essence, the ability to be moulded by the moves of the partner.

If you look carefully, you will notice that an overriding desire to **"please others"** runs through the whole passage quoted above. First, Herodias' daughter danced to please Herod; in other words, she made herself available as a "**servant**" or "maid" ready to please Herod with her dance moves. Then, Herod felt a desire to please her back, telling her to request anything from him; in other words, Herod made himself available as a "servant" ready to please her back by giving her the gift she desired. Then, instead of thinking about what **she** wanted from the king, Herodias' daughter quickly ran to her mother to see what **Herodias** wanted; in other words, the daughter saw the king's words as an opportunity to please her mother. When her mother said that she wanted the head of John the Baptist, Herodias' daughter did not pause to consider if such a request was morally correct or if it was **pleasing to God**; she was so concerned about "pleasing mummy" that she returned to the king and asked for John the Baptist's head on a platter. Herod did not want to kill John (v26), but he was so concerned about pleasing Herodias' daughter and "what people might think" that he simply acquiesced to her petition and told his executioner to bring him the head of John the Baptist. Notice how everyone was trying to please everyone else in this passage, and notice how the Canaanite desire to please people can be so strong that you end up doing things your convictions wouldn't normally allow you to do. Canaanites create a type of "**peer-pressure**" atmosphere that make convictions subservient to the desires of men. **People under Canaanite influence are constantly worried about what people might think.**

Why did Herodias request John the Baptist's head on a **platter**? The word translated as "charger" by the King James translators in Mark 6:25 and Mark 6:28 is the Greek word *pinax*, which means, "a board, a dish, a platter", and apparently is derived from the Greek word *plax*, meaning, "a flat thing, a level surface". The word *plax* itself comes from the Greek word *plasso*, which means, "to form, to mould". From this, we can see several connexions with things previously said in this chapter:

❑ As we said above, Genesis 13 relates the Hebrew word for "plain" with one of the Hebrew words for "dancing", and the Greek word *plax* means "a flat thing, a level surface", which is very much related to the concept of a "plain".

❑ As we said above, Aaron moulded a golden calf to the liking of the children of Israel in order to please them and give them the "God" they wanted. This relates to the word *plasso*, which means "to form, to mould". When we fall under a Canaanite influence, we start dancing to the desires of others and become like spiritual "plains", lowlands that have been "moulded" into spiritual flatness by the desires of men instead of allowing God to mould us and shape us.

Platters are used by waiters, implying that John's head was brought in the same way that a waiter would bring food as a service to satisfy the desires of a customer. **An important quality in a good servant or "maid" is the desire to please the person being served.** This is why people who are born with the Spirit of Service are very prone to falling under the influence of Canaanite spirits; in an effort to serve others, these people sometimes throw personal convictions out the window when these convictions get in the way of the other person's service request. Having a Spirit of Service is not wrong in and of itself. In fact, the Spirit of Service is one of the 7 Spirits of God (Revelation 3:1, 4:5). The 7 Spirits of God correspond to the 7 churches mentioned at the beginning of the book of Revelation; the 7 spirits of evil that we are studying in this series are, in fact, the corruptions of each of the seven spirits of God. We will be publishing future books on this, God willing, but, for now, we give a **brief** list of the **7 spirits of God** and their spiritual "opposites" or "corrupted images" in the world of iniquity:

Brief List of the 7 Spirits of God[17]

Spirit of God	Church in Rev 2 & 3	Related ministry	Jehovah Name	Attributes the Spirit of God imbues us with	Evil corruptions
Spirit of Judgement	Ephesus	Apostles	Tsidkenu (Jer. 33:16)	Wisdom to judge	Jebusites
Spirit of Self-sacrifice	Smyrna	Prophets	Shamah (Eze. 48:35)	Willingness to die for others	Hittites
Spirit of Head authority	Pergamos	Evangelists	Rophe (Exo. 15:26)	Ability to conquer in the spirit world	Amorites
Spirit of Service	Thyatira	Pastors	Jireh (Gen. 22:14)	Desire to serve and to please	Canaanites
Spirit of Perfection	Sardis	Teachers	Makkadesh (Lev. 22:32)	Desire to complete what is missing	Girgashites
Spirit of Dreams & Visions	Philadelphia	---	Nissi (Exo. 17:15)	Visions of great things whilst still being small	Perizzites
Spirit of Prosperity	Laodicea	---	Shalom (Jdg. 6:24)	Abundance and judgement-based *shalom* peace	Hivites

When studying the seven Spirits of God, it becomes evident that the Spirit of Service is very strong on people with **pastoral callings** on their lives; this is also backed by simple observation of people in whom the pastoral calling is very evident. Those of you who have a strong desire to serve and please others were definitely born to be pastors, and are very probably **already** working as pastors in the spirit realm, even if you don't currently work full-time as a "pastor" at some congregation. The Church is so literal in its understanding of God's Word that it has not grasped the fact that pastoring is a **spiritual** activity, not a physical one. I am fully convinced (and I write this knowing that God is reading what I am writing) that **all** believers are born with **at least** one of the five ministries of Ephesians 4:11. The

---

[17] You may read more on the 7 Spirits of God in a "Question & Answer" posting titled "What are the 7 sins and virtues?" posted on the Shamah-Elim website (http://shamah-elim.info/qa/q_7sinsvirt.htm).

Bible very clearly declares that **all** of us who have given our hearts to the Anointed One (Christ) are priests and ministers of God (Revelation 1:6, Isaiah 61:6), and, as such, we all have gifts and ministries that are to be manifested on Earth. Many of you who are pastors in the eyes of God are carrying out your pastoral ministry at the place where you work, at home, or at the place where you study. Your mere presence wherever God sends you exerts a pastoral influence on the spiritual atmosphere around you, and you are affecting people's spiritual lives through your pastoral anointing, even if you are not audibly preaching a sermon from a pulpit. This not only applies to pastors but to all ministries. Those of you who have a prophetic calling on your life are probably already engaging in spiritual battle against Hittite, Jebusite, and Amorite spirits; your presence wherever God has you at this moment is exerting a prophetic influence on the believers and unbelievers that surround you. You don't have to be "**ordained**" by a pastor in front of a congregation to be recognised by God as a prophet. My friend, you **already are** a prophet. You were a prophet when you were in your mother's womb, before you were even born!!! (Jeremiah 1:5)

Those of you who were born with the Spirit of Service must be very careful not to be controlled by Canaanite spirits. You have a natural, God-given predisposition to please others, and, it is very likely that you have a hard time saying "no" to people's requests. Be careful not to get so caught up in dancing for others that you end up serving up a prophet's head on a platter.

It is worth clarifying that **Canaanite spirits distort the emotions in us that wish to please others**. Hittites spirits deceive us about whom or what we are to die for, whilst Canaanite spirits deceive us about whom or what we are to live for and serve.

Dancing means to "get down"

The word "Canaan" means, "lowland" in Hebrew, and is derived from another Hebrew word, *kana*, which means, "to be humble, to be brought down". This makes spiritual sense, since you must be willing to humiliate yourself if you want to serve them. Remember how the Lord Jesus washed the disciple's feet (John 13). Service and humiliation go hand in hand:

"*4Look not every man on his own things, but every man also on the things of others. 5Let this mind be in you, which was also in Christ Jesus: 6Who, being in the form of God, thought it not* robbery to be equal with God: ^{7}But **made himself of no reputation**, and **took upon him the form of a servant**, and was made in the likeness of men: ^{8}And being found in fashion as a man, he humbled himself, and became obedient unto death, even the death of the cross." (Philippians 2:4-8)

Those of you who have been asked to dance on stage in front of an audience probably know how embarrassing it is to dance for others (especially if "ants in his pants" is the phrase that comes to people's minds when they see you dance). Dancing, literal and spiritual, is a public exposition of weakness in order to please others. It's no wonder that people use the phrase "getting down" when referring to dancing.

Those of you with the Spirit of Service don't mind dancing and humiliating yourselves in front of others. You don't mind girding yourself with a towel to wash other people's feet (John 13:4), as long as that humiliation blesses them. **By nature, you are prone to deriving pleasure from pleasing other people.** If you are not careful, however, your dancing may turn from a "sacrifice pleasant unto God" into a Canaanite dance that is an abomination to Him.

Don't dance for pigs and dogs

Don't dance to please the desires of pigs and dogs. They don't appreciate your service and sacrifice, and you are only "validating" and solidifying their iniquity when you continue to fulfil their doggish and piggish desires. **Canaanite believers, in their zeal to please others, are prone to giving people more than they need or deserve.**

"Give not that which is holy unto the dogs, neither cast ye your pearls before swine, lest they trample them under their feet, and turn again and rend you." (Matthew 7:6)

Even though the Gospel calls us to a life of suffering in service and self-sacrifice, not all suffering is necessarily of God:

"^{14}If ye be reproached for the name of Christ, happy are ye; for the spirit of glory and of God resteth upon you: on their part he is evil spoken of, but on your part he is glorified. ^{15}But **let none of you suffer as a murderer, or as a thief, or as an evildoer, or as a busybody in other men's matters.** ^{16}Yet if any man suffer as a Christian, let him not be ashamed; but let him glorify God on this behalf. ^{17}For the time is come that judgment must begin at the house of God: and if it first begin at *us, what shall the end be of them that obey not the gospel of God?" (1 Peter 4:14-17)*

The phrase "busybody in other men's matters" in verse 15 above was translated from the Greek word *allotriepiskopos*, which literally means, "one who supervises a stranger's affairs". In other words, it refers to investing your service in things that serve the interests of another master besides your own. You and I are, before all things, **God**'s servants, not **man**'s servants, and we are called to serve man in whatsoever serves the purpose of our Master, the Lord Jesus. When our service promotes the kingdom of another "master", the word "*allotri-episkopos*" applies to us. If our service does not work as seed to produce **fruits of righteousness** in others, working instead to strengthen or condone their iniquity, it becomes useless service in the eyes of God:

*"[9]As it is written, He hath dispersed abroad; he hath given to the poor: his righteousness remaineth for ever. [10]Now he that ministereth seed to the sower both minister bread for your food, and multiply your seed sown, and **increase the fruits of your righteousness**" (2 Corinthians 9:9-10)*

*"[9](For **the fruit of the Spirit is in all goodness and righteousness and truth**;) [10]Proving what is **acceptable unto the Lord**." (Ephesians 5:9-10)*

The word translated as "goodness" in Ephesians 5:9 above is the Greek word *agathosune*, which refers to "**uprightness**" and "**integrity**", and not to "kindness and mercy", as the word "goodness" is sometimes taken to mean in English and other languages. The word translated as "acceptable" in Ephesians 5:10 above is the Greek word *euarestos*, which literally means, "well-pleasing". This implies that what pleases God are those things that are full of integrity, justice (i.e.- "righteousness"), and truth. As we mentioned in the chapter on the Hittites[18], God writes from right to left, meaning that His giving and His grace (which is left-handed) flows out of a foundation of truth and justice (which are right-handed). If a service or gift is not truth-based, it becomes purposeless and vain in the eyes of God, and His eyes are the Ones that count at the end.

---

[18] pg. 66

Pleasing that pleases God

The Lord sets very clear parameters to determine if our pleasing of others is pleasing to Him:

"³¹Whether therefore ye eat, or drink, or whatsoever ye do, do all to the glory of God. ³²Give none offence, neither to the Jews, nor to the Gentiles, nor to the church of God: ³³Even as I please all men in all things, not seeking mine own profit, but the profit of many, that they may be saved." (1 Corinthians 10:31-33)

In verse 31, Paul declares that we must do all things to the glory of God. If it does not bring God glory, it must not be done, and the only things that bring Him Glory are those that are in His **will, righteousness, and purpose.** Everything else is vain and pointless (Matthew 12:30, Psalm 127:1-5).

In verse 33 of the passage quoted above, Paul adds that his desire to please all men is constrained by two parameters:

❑ **Selflessness** ("not seeking my own profit")
This means that there must be no selfish interests or hidden agendas in my pleasing of others. I must give of myself selflessly.

❑ **Salvation in others** ("that they may be saved")
The word translated as "saved" in verse 33 is the Greek word *sozo*, which has the connotation of "restoration" or "redemption from destruction". All salvation or redemption in Scripture is **judgement-based.** When we are saved from going to hell, we have to repent and accept God's judgement against us. We must accept the label of "sinner" and "condemned" in order to be saved (John 16:8, Acts 2:32-41). Otherwise, there will be no repentance, and, hence, no salvation from hell. Since salvation in Scripture is described as a **process** that **starts** when you and I are **born** again (Philippians 2:12-13), we must understand that **total** salvation is the restoration of **all** which man lost when he sinned against God, which implies a growth process; therefore, it also implies growing pains (Hebrews 12:4-13). The word in Hebrew for "process", *mishpat*, is the same word for "judgement". This confirms the fact that salvation in the lives of others comes through the application of **spiritual** judgements (not carnal judgements) that work to produce righteousness in the other person. If my pleasing of others does not work towards producing righteousness in them, it is not working towards their salvation. If my pleasing of another person is done to shield that

person pain and suffering that he or she **needs** to go through in order to have fruits of righteousness produced in him or her, I am working towards the **destruction** of that person, not the person's salvation (Proverbs 23:14, 13:24, 29:15; Matthew 18:15; James 5:19-20, 2 Corinthians 7:8-11).

Sometimes, allow others to dance for you

Those with a Spirit of Service find it easy to serve or "get down" for others, but find it difficult or uncomfortable to have others "get down" or dance for them. This is why Simon Peter, who had a **pastoral** calling on his life besides his apostolic and evangelistic calling (John 21:15-18), did not want Jesus to wash his feet:

*"⁶Then cometh he to Simon Peter: and Peter saith unto him, **Lord, dost thou wash my feet?** ⁷Jesus answered and said unto him, What I do thou knowest not now; but thou shalt know hereafter. ⁸Peter saith unto him, Thou shalt never wash my feet. Jesus answered him, If I wash thee not, thou hast no part with me." (John 13:6-8)*

Sometimes those with a true pastoral calling on their lives feel uncomfortable about others "dancing" to please **them**, even if God was the One who appointed that "dancing", as was the case with the Lord Jesus in John chapter 13. Jesus, who had the Spirit of Service (along with all the seven Spirits of God), allowed a woman at one time to "get down" in front of Him to wash and anoint His feet with her hair (Luke 7:36-49; notice the reference to "dancing" in Luke 7:32-34). From time to time, allow others to dance for you, and be grateful to them for it, but never allow anyone to dance for you when they have **not** been sent by God to do so. You will be opening a door for pride in your life and allowing the other person to perform **self-deprecation** that will **curse** that person's life, instead of blessing him or her:

*"And **I fell at his feet to worship him**. And **he said unto me, See thou do it not: I am thy fellowservant**, and of thy brethren that have the testimony of Jesus: worship God: for the testimony of Jesus is the spirit of prophecy." (Revelation 19:10)*

*"²⁵And as Peter was coming in, **Cornelius** met him, and **fell down at his feet**, and worshipped him. ²⁶But Peter took him up, saying, **Stand up; I myself also am a man**." (Acts 10:25-26)*

Curse the Canaanites

When Israel was about to enter into the Promised Land to conquer it, they first had to fight against Arad, a Canaanite king, and against Sihon and Og, two Amorite kings (Numbers chapter 21). Before fighting against the Canaanites, Israel did an interesting thing:

*"¹And when king **Arad the Canaanite,** which dwelt in the south, heard tell that Israel came by the way of the spies; then he fought against Israel, and took some of them prisoners. ²And Israel vowed a vow unto the LORD, and said, **If thou wilt indeed deliver this people into my hand, then I will utterly destroy their cities**. ³And the LORD hearkened to the voice of Israel, and delivered up the Canaanites; and they utterly destroyed them and their cities: and he called the name of the place Hormah"* (Numbers 21:1-3)

This illustrates a "simple" but important principle that is essential to overcoming Canaanite spirits in your own life and in the collective lives of others: **you must condemn the Canaanites to destruction with the words of your mouth**. The name "Hormah" mentioned at the end of the passage above means, "devoted unto destruction" or "set apart to be destroyed". If you are struggling with a Canaanite addiction in your life, you must be willing to commit yourself to its total destruction, without compromises. One gets entangled in Canaanite addictions because of **compromise**, i.e.- because of having cast aside your convictions in order to please other people. This means that you must be willing to **cut off all relationship** with anything or **anyone** that *promotes or harbours* the Canaanite spirit. This is why Israel made a vow to destroy the *Canaanites' cities*. Human reasoning would have said that it made more sense to simply overcome the Canaanites and take advantage of their houses and their animals. However, it is impossible to truly defeat them in the Spirit if you are not willing to commit yourself to their total destruction, in your life and in the lives of others. Once you make the commitment in your heart and curse the Canaanites and all their "safe havens" unto destruction, God Himself will come and fight through you and give you **total** victory over them.

The world is currently infested with Canaanite spirits of pornography, sexual immorality, drug and alcohol addictions, and other deviant practices. You and I, as believers, must pray in the Spirit, sending out judgement word into the air from our prayer closets to condemn and destroy these Canaanite spirits. Most believers seem to think that the key to victory is to write to their MPs or Congressmen, pressuring them into passing laws that legislate morality. This is the human approach, and it will never, **never** work. This is a spiritual battle, and the battle must be fought with spiritual weapons. The consequences in the natural realm will then take care of themselves.

Pray for judgement against all those who do pornographic movies. Pray for the vial of destructive and grievous sores to be poured over their lives (each of the 7 vials of wrath in Revelation 16 corresponds to each of the 7 types of evil spirits; the first vial corresponds to the Canaanites). Pray for disease, sadness and grief to bear over the lives of pornographic actors when they sleep at night. Pray for them to find no peace whatsoever until they recognise their sins and expose their lives to the cleansing effect of Jesus's blood. Pray for drug dealers to be grieved with disease and heartache, to be without any rest or peace in their lives until they either repent or are killed. Some of these people are so hardened in their hearts that they will never repent; they only stay around on Earth to contaminate and destroy the lives of more and more people, so, in those cases, it is better for them to die. Obviously, it is not about you killing them literally! It is through spiritual warfare, through **prayer**, that these things will happen. The prophetic remnant of the latter days will be a "no-holds-barred" type of Church, a Church that will unleash punishing and unrelenting spiritual warfare against iniquity, paving the way for the greatest revival mankind has ever seen.

People who have a strong manifestation of God's Spirit of Service are very sociable people and are very prone to valuing **social relationships** and **human contact**. This is the reason why most pastors (who by definition have the Spirit of Service) tend to be friendly people who like to have contact with people. Sometimes, this "contact" is so literal that they always like to go around hugging people, patting people on the shoulder, shaking hands, etc. This desire for human contact, however, can lead people to value their soulish relationships more than they value the laws and the justice of God. For example, a young lady might be so in love with a young man who is touching her improperly that she prefers to expose her body to his fornicating hands than to lose her relationship with him. In a sense, she prefers to "dance" for him and please him than to please God, because pleasing God would imply losing soul-contact with that young man. By not condemning the Canaanite spirit inside of her to destruction, and by not confronting the young man over his filthy behaviour, she is doing him more harm than good; he will not understand that he is sinning against God until he is **confronted**.

Another example of how people with the Spirit of Service might value relationships over God's justice would be when a pastor likes a brother so much that he (or she) is not willing to confront that person, even if the brother is deliberately committing great sin against God. Remember how Peter, who was a pastor, confronted Ananias and Sapphira, pronouncing word of judgement against them that **killed** them, even though the "only" thing they did was lie to God (Acts 5:1-11). Peter was more interested in executing God's judgements on Earth than on preserving his soul-relationship with them.

Another **painfully common** example of how people with the Spirit of Service might value relationships over God's justice would be when a mother "loves" a son so much that she bends over backwards to help him out of problems caused by his deliberate choice to live a life of sin and unrighteousness. Many mothers make great personal sacrifices to support their adult sons out of financial difficulties, for example, even when those financial problems are caused by irresponsible and sinful behaviour such as alcohol and drug addiction. These mothers are motivated by left-handed, emotional love that is not based on a right-hand mind of judgement and truth. They refuse to confront their sons out of fear of losing "soul contact" with them.

"The rod and reproof give wisdom: but a child left to himself bringeth his mother to shame." (Proverbs 29:15)

"[13]Withhold not correction from the child: for if thou beatest him with the rod, he shall not die. [14]Thou shalt beat him with the rod, and shalt deliver his soul from hell." (Proverbs 23:13-14)

The word translated as "hell" in the passage above is the Hebrew word "Sheol", which refers to hell in a literal sense and to "purposelessness" in a spiritual sense. Hell is like a big wheelie bin where things that are **no longer useful** are thrown away to be burned. When someone loses his or her prophetic calling in life due to deliberate hard-heartedness, his or her **prophetic purpose** is lost; he or she becomes useless, in a spiritual sense, and, once that happens, it is equivalent to having his or her calling cast into the fire of Sheol (by the way, if you fear that you have lost your prophetic calling, and if the mere thought of that causes pain in your heart, then your calling is not yet lost; those who lose their calling become so callous that they simply don't care). Therefore, when the Bible refers to Sheol or "hell", it is referring, in a spiritual sense, to a life that has strayed from its prophetic purpose and is no longer useful. When a mother refuses to apply judgement and justice out of fear of losing her soulish relationship with her son, she is allowing the prophetic calling of that son to be cast into the fire of hell. If the son did not receive Jesus as his Saviour, he will end up in hell along with his prophetic calling. If he did receive Jesus as his Saviour, he will escape hell literally, but his prophetic calling will be lost, and, the day he faces God, he will understand all the **eternal** things that he gave up for the sake of temporary things, and he will be **vomited out by God** (Revelation 3:14-22), cast away from God's presence forever, even if he himself does not "physically" end up in hell. He will "exist" eternally, but will not be allowed to eat from the tree of life. Canaanite mother, are you willing to let all of this happen because this short life would be "too painful" without your son near you? You must be willing to curse the Canaanite spirit in you, confront your son in his iniquity, and curse the iniquity in him unto destruction. Your hands will then be free from the responsibility of his blood, because you will have warned him in time and acted in God's righteousness (Ezekiel 33:1-11).

Without cursing the Canaanites, there can be no true victory against them.

So much more to say

There is so much more left to say about the Canaanite spirits!! Scripture reveals a strong association between Canaanites and dogs, as well as an association between Canaanites and vengeful judgements inspired by misguided emotionalism and not by a zeal for God's righteousness. Canaanites abhor God's righteous judgements, and they are the foundational force behind the man-made barriers that fight to keep God's judgements and justice from permeating the Earth. The Canaanites' emotional effort, however, shall fail, for it is written that unrighteousness shall not prevail (Psalm 105:1-7, Proverbs 12:19).

To learn more about Canaanite spirits, we recommend the following postings from the Shamah-Elim Bible Studies website:

+ Article "The real Unity of the Church" (http://shamah-elim.info/unity.htm)
+ Article "Wolves in the Church" (http://shamah-elim.info/wolves.htm)
+ Article "Pastoral evangelism" (http://shamah-elim.info/pastevan.htm)
+ Prophetic word "The broken EU net" (http://shamah-elim.info/p_brokeneu.htm)
+ Prophetic word "Frogs in the Church" (http://shamah-elim.info/p_frogs.htm)
+ Question & Answer "Curse the Canaanites" (http://shamah-elim.info/qa/q_cursecan.htm)

Chapter 6
The Perizzites

This chapter will focus on the "Perizzites". These are the spirits that perpetuate the need for a "crutch", i.e.- the need to permanently depend on others. As the Jebusites, the Girgashites, and the Amorites carry out their oppression, they lay the groundwork for the entry of these Perizzite spirits that "seal the deal" on the oppressive work of the other spirits. The Perizzite spirit promotes a sense of permanent shame and inadequacy, and it robs people of their ability to dream.

An article similar to this chapter is posted on the Shamah-Elim Bible Studies website at the following web address:
http://shamah-elim.info/perizite.htm

What's in a name?

A great deal can be inferred directly from the meaning of the word "Perizzite", which means, "belonging to a village". Villages have a connotation of "smallness". People who grow up in villages are exposed to very limited opportunities for growth; educational, cultural, and entertainment opportunities are scarce. If they are not careful, people who grow up in villages can develop a very **limited vision** of life. Dreams are easily spawned in an environment that stimulates people with options and opportunities; since these are limited in a village, villagers are very **likely not to dream of great things**, and the few who do, dream of making it out of the village in order to succeed in the big cities. Frank Sinatra's "New York, New York" song, therefore, would be an example of an "anti-Perizzite" song, for it speaks of walking into great things and places of great opportunities.

Since villages impart a sense of "smallness", "villagers" (both literal and figurative) tend to see themselves as **small and insignificant people** who are a tiny part of a small and insignificant community. People trapped by the Perizzite spirit, therefore, see themselves as people with **little potential** whose only missions in life are to live out a quiet biological existence and to stay out of the way of the people who are "really" important in this world. Perizzites not only believe in their **own** smallness, but also believe in the smallness of the "villagers" around them, including their children. The Perizzite spirit, therefore, can lead to **many generations of spiritual stagnation.**

Since stagnation always leads to poverty (in the material and in the spiritual realm), Perizzite spirits tend to produce **many generations of spiritual (and even literal) poverty**.

Perizzites are "Tiny Tims"

The Lord declares that Jonathan, Saul's son, had a son named Mephibosheth who was crippled by the nurse who took care of him. This happened as she fled with him upon learning that Saul and Jonathan had died in battle. She fled out of fear that the new king would want to kill all members of Saul's "royal family":

"And Jonathan, Saul's son, had a son that was lame of his feet. **He was five years old** *when the tidings came of Saul and Jonathan out of Jezreel, and his nurse took him up, and fled: and it came to pass,* **as she made haste to flee, that he fell, and became lame.** *And his name was Mephibosheth"* (2 Samuel 4:4)

Since David loved Mephibosheth's father, Jonathan, David wanted to bless Mephibosheth, and called him to his presence:

"⁵Then king David sent, and fetched him out of the house of Machir, the son of Ammiel, from Lodebar. ⁶Now when Mephibosheth, the son of Jonathan, the son of Saul, was come unto David, he fell on his face, and did reverence. And David said, Mephibosheth. **And he answered, Behold thy servant!** *⁷And* **David said unto him, Fear not: for I will surely shew thee kindness for Jonathan thy father's sake,** *and will restore thee all the land of Saul thy father; and thou shalt eat bread at my table continually. ⁸And he bowed himself, and said,* **What is thy servant, that thou shouldest look upon such a dead dog as I am?"** *(2 Samuel 9:5-8)*

Because of his disability, Mephibosheth grew up to be a person with a **very low self-esteem**. Notice how Mephibosheth, even after hearing David's gracious words, refers to himself as a "dead dog" (v8). Perizzites are cripples, lame people who feel unworthy, who feel spiritually unable to walk on their own.

"Walking" in Scripture is a spiritual figure of the ability to conquer and to establish **kingdom authority**:

"²Moses my servant is dead; now therefore arise, go over this Jordan, thou, and all this people, unto the land which I do give to

them, even to the children of Israel. *³Every place that the sole of your foot shall tread upon, that have I given unto you*, as I said unto Moses." (Joshua 1:2-3)

"*¹⁷Arise, **walk through the land** in the length of it and in the breadth of it; for **I will give it unto thee**. ¹⁸Then Abram removed his tent, and came and dwelt in the plain of Mamre, which is in Hebron, and built there an altar unto the LORD."* (Genesis 13:17-18)

"Walking" in Scripture also refers to the ability to judge:

"*⁶In the days of Shamgar the son of Anath, in the days of Jael, the highways were unoccupied, and the travellers walked through byways. ⁷The inhabitants of the villages ceased, they ceased in Israel, until that I Deborah arose, that I arose a mother in Israel. ⁸They chose new gods; then was war in the gates: was there a shield or spear seen among forty thousand in Israel? ⁹My heart is toward the governors of Israel, that offered themselves willingly among the people. Bless ye the LORD. ¹⁰Speak, ye that ride on white asses, **ye that sit in judgment, and walk by the way**. ¹¹They that are delivered from the noise of archers in the places of drawing water, there shall they rehearse the righteous acts of the LORD, even the righteous acts toward the inhabitants of his villages in Israel: then shall the people of the LORD go down to the gates."* (Judges 5:6-11)

Notice how verse 6 above refers to people not walking freely on "highways" and how verse 7 refers to "villages" (perazown in Hebrew), which establishes the spiritual connexion between Perizzites and the inability to walk freely. Verse 10 then refers to those that "sit in judgement" and "walk by the way". This means that "walking" is tied in Scripture to **the ability to make judgements**. This is why verse 11 refers to the victory of God's "villages" in Israel and to the people of the Lord going down to the "gates". This refers to God's "little, village people" making judgements, since ancient cities placed their "tribunals" or "courts" at the city's "gates". This relationship between walking and making judgements is reinforced in other passages of Scripture:

"*And David my servant shall be king over them; and they all shall have one shepherd: they shall also **walk in my judgments**, and observe my statutes, and do them."* (Ezekiel 37:24)

*"And I will put my spirit within you, and cause you to **walk in my statutes, and ye shall keep my judgments**, and do them." (Ezekiel 36:27)*

*"Ye shall **do my judgments**, and keep mine ordinances, to **walk therein**: I am the LORD your God." (Leviticus 18:4)*

*"¹¹And the word of the LORD came to Solomon, saying, ¹²Concerning this house which thou art in building, **if thou wilt walk in my statutes, and execute my judgments**, and keep all my commandments to walk in them; then will I perform my word with thee, which I spake unto David thy father:" (1 Kings 6:11-12)*

"Walking in His judgements" implies an ability to know what those judgements are. This is why Scripture also relates "walking" to remaining before God's Face:

*"Therefore now, LORD God of Israel, keep with thy servant David my father that thou promisedst him, saying, There shall not fail thee a man in my sight to sit on the throne of Israel; so that thy children take heed to their way, that they walk before me as **thou hast walked before me**." (1 Kings 8:25)*

*"And if thou wilt **walk before me**, as David thy father walked, in integrity of heart, and in uprightness, to do according to all that I have commanded thee, and wilt keep my statutes and **my judgments**" (1 Kings 9:4)*

*"And as for thee, if thou wilt **walk before me**, as David thy father walked, and do according to all that I have commanded thee, and shalt observe my statutes and **my judgments**" (2 Chronicles 7:17)*

In all the verses above, the word translated as "before" in phrases such as "walk before Me" is the Hebrew word *paniym*, which literally means "face". Therefore, the phrase "to walk before the Lord" literally means, "to walk before the face of the Lord". In Scripture, seeing a person "face to face" implies a **direct relationship** with that person. This is why we, as believers, are called to **make judgements**, because we have a direct relationship with the Lawgiver Himself. We have been given the mind of Christ (1 Corinthians 2:15-16), meaning that we have an ability to hear from God and to discern His laws and spiritual principles. Since "walking" is related to making judgements and to having a direct relationship with God, we can infer that Perizzites, who are spiritual cripples, are people who believe that they do not have the authority or the ability to make spiritual judgements. As spiritual cripples, Perizzite believers refuse to "walk", and prefer to delegate spiritual judgements to those whom they believe to be more "deserving" of such an honour than their "tiny" and "insignificant" selves. This creates a relationship of **spiritual dependency** between the crippled Perizzite believer and those whom he or she considers to be of a higher "spiritual caste".

I am so saddened when I hear believers say, "Who am I to judge?". By saying this, they are admitting that they are spiritually crippled, unable to walk in God's judgements and denying a direct relationship between themselves and God the Father. Many take the famous words in Matthew 7:1, "Judge not, that ye be not judged" as a spiritual excuse to remain in their spiritual lameness. However, they are taking these words out of their true spiritual context, since the same Jesus who pronounced these words says the following later on:

*"Judge not according to the appearance, but **judge righteous judgment.**" (John 7:24)*

If "judging" is inherently wrong, why would the Lord Jesus tell us to "judge righteous judgement" in the passage above? Why would Paul, under the anointing of the Spirit, say the following to the believers in Corinth?

*"[1]It is reported commonly that there is fornication among you, and such fornication as is not so much as named among the Gentiles, that one should have his father's wife. [2]And ye are puffed up, and have not rather mourned, that he that hath done this deed might be taken away from among you. [3]For **I verily, as absent in body, but present in spirit, have judged already, as though I were present, concerning him that hath so done this deed,** [4]In the name of our Lord Jesus Christ, when ye are gathered together, and my spirit, with the power of our Lord Jesus Christ, [5]To **deliver such an one unto satan for the destruction of the flesh**, that the spirit may be saved in the day of the Lord Jesus. [6]Your glorying is not good. Know ye not that a little leaven leaveneth the whole lump?" (1 Corinthians 5:1-6)*

If "judging" is inherently wrong, why would Paul say in verse 3 above that he has already "judged that person" (the word "concerning" that appears in verse 3 does not appear in the original Greek text, and was added by the King James translators as a "buffer" word because, to their natural minds, it sounded inappropriate to faithfully translate that Paul had **judged** another human being). After verse 3, Paul proceeds to tell the Corinthians to deliver the sinning believer unto satan (v5). A few verses later, in 1 Corinthians 5:12, he reprimands them for **not judging** those within the Church. Does all of the above sound as if judging was a sin? Obviously not!

Why then, did the Lord say "judge not" in Matthew 7:1? Because He was speaking to **souls** at the time, not to **spirits**. The entire "Sermon on the Mount", of which Matthew 7:1 is a part, focuses on **submission of the soul to the spirit.** This is why the Sermon begins with a reference to Jesus "seeing the multitudes" in Matthew 5:1; in Scripture, "multitudes" generally refer to crowds of souls (compare Revelation 6:9-11 with Revelation 7:9). The Sermon then proceeds to talk about soulish concerns such as food and shelter (the word translated as "life" in Matthew 6:25, for example, is the Greek word *psyche*, which is the same word in Greek for "soul"). The only time that the word "spirit" is mentioned by Jesus in the Sermon on the Mount is in Matthew 5:3, where He said, "poor in spirit", referring to those who are reduced to a state of "beggary" as punishment by the world for abiding in the Spirit. Since the Word declares that our **spirits** are rich (1 Corinthians 1:5, 2 Corinthians 6:10, Revelation 2:9), the "poverty" of Matthew 5:3 is referring to poverty of the soul, not the spirit. This means that, even when Jesus mentions the word "spirit" in the Sermon on the Mount, He is talking to our souls, not our spirits.

Therefore, we can conclude that Jesus is ordering our **souls** not to judge in Matthew 7:1. Our spirits, on the contrary, are **called** to make judgements. Otherwise, we would have to tear out many passages from our Bibles:

"[15]But **he that is spiritual judgeth all things,** yet he himself is judged of no man. [16]For who hath known the mind of the Lord, that he may instruct him? But **we have the mind of Christ**." (1 Corinthians 2:15-16)

"God standeth in the congregation of the mighty; **he judgeth among the gods**" (Psalm 82:1)

"[34]Jesus answered them, Is it not written in your law, I said, Ye are gods? [35]If he called them gods, unto whom the word of God came, and the scripture cannot be broken ..." (John 10:34-35)

*"22But ye are come unto mount Sion, and unto the city of the living God, the heavenly Jerusalem, and to an innumerable company of angels, 23To the general assembly and church of the firstborn, which are written in heaven, and **to God the Judge of all**, and **to the spirits of just men made perfect**" (Hebrews 12:22-23)*

When we judge in the soul, we judge according to laws devised by our souls according to our own interests and natural understanding. When we judge in the Spirit, we judge not according to our own laws but according to the Laws of God. We become impartial judges who apply His Laws using the mind of Christ, which goes beyond external appearances and can discern the deep things of the heart and mind that are completely invisible to our natural minds (1 Corinthians 2:14-16, Hebrews 4:12).

Perizzite believers are unaware of their spiritual authority to judge, and, therefore, they are to God as spiritual cripples, unable to walk in His judgements and unable to establish God's kingdom authority on Earth. As I was preparing to write this chapter (on 3 July 2004), I heard the Lord say the phrase "Tiny Tim" to my right ear. To be honest with you, I really did not know who "Tiny Tim" was, even though I had heard the name before. The Lord then told me to search the Internet to find out who Tiny Tim was, and, as I did, I stumbled upon a story about a little baby who survived an abortion (I found this story at aprisonerofhope.com and faithfulhope.com, but these sites were later deactivated). I also learnt that "Tiny Tim" was the name of a character in Dickens' story, "A Christmas Carol" (I guess I did not know about "Tiny Tim" because, for a long time, I have been against Christmas, since its historical origins are pagan, and it is not Biblically based, and no matter how good our intentions may be, **Jesus** did not command us to celebrate Christmas; that is **man** trying to find a human way to please God, and God abhors that; Christmas was a humanly devised mechanism to get pagans to convert to Christianity; if you do not agree, I encourage you to please do research on the origins of Christmas and to pray to God that He show you the spiritual underpinnings of Christmas, and to make a judgement on your own, in the Spirit).

From what I found on the Internet regarding "Tiny Tim", I understood why the Lord whispered this phrase to me when I was preparing to write this chapter. Tiny Tim was a *crippled* child in Dickens' story, and the aborted baby named "Tiny Tim" was a young human being who was considered insignificant by his mum, but who was **very** important in God's eyes (from what I read, I understood that Tiny Tim's mum has repented from what she did, so God has forgiven her). Unfortunately, the Church today is full of Tiny Tims, full of believers whose spiritual calling dies before it gets the opportunity to grow and blossom. Why? Because they buy into the doctrine that preaches the greatness of the "minister" and the littleness of "regular church folks". They buy into the doctrine that says that only full-time ministers can make spiritual judgements and that they are to sit quietly in their pews and take in all that is told to them, without the right to judge what they hear. It angers Almighty God to have a Church ruled by pastors who have denied believers the right to have direct access to God the Lawgiver, to God the Father; these pastors stand as **permanent** (not **temporary**) intermediaries between God and the rest of mankind (1 Peter 5:2-3, Matthew 19:6, Galatians 3:19-29). Even though the Church claims to be living in New Testament grace, most of it still believes (spiritually speaking) in the intermediaries of the Old Testament, convinced that only the "Aaronic" priests (i.e.- full-time ministers) have a direct access to the Holy Place and to the Holy of Holies. It grieves and angers God to see a Church full of Perizzite cripples, full of Tiny Tims who are dependent upon man and not directly upon Him, but God has prophesied in His word that the days of these "Aaronic" priests are numbered, and that a mighty people, an awe-inspiring spiritual Church will be raised up in these last days to manifest His Glory on Earth (Zechariah 8:1-23, Micah 7:1-20). This will be a **walking** remnant, not crippled by man, but empowered with the Anointing of the Holy Spirit.

This word is for the Christian Church in the United States:

> *You have made mighty human efforts to abolish abortion from your land, but you will not have spiritual authority to abolish it until you drive out the Perizzites that are inside My Church, says the Lord. I will not give you victory over the enemy outside until you defeat him inside. Stop aborting the spiritual callings of My people, and stop crippling their spiritual authority. My times of judgement are now, says the Lord, and I will roar like a furious lion against those who have crippled My people. I will come against them and tear them to shreds, says the Lord, for I am an awesome God, and the zeal for My people consumes Me.*

Who crippled the Perizzites?

To answer the above question, we have to go back and see how Mephibosheth was crippled:

"And Jonathan, Saul's son, had a son that was lame of his feet. **He was five years old** *when the tidings came of Saul and Jonathan out of Jezreel, and his nurse took him up, and fled: and it came to pass, as she made haste to flee, that he fell, and became lame. And his name was Mephibosheth"* (2 Samuel 4:4)

The Holy Spirit points out that Mephibosheth was **5** years old when he was left crippled. Why "5"? Because "5" is a number that refers to **ministerial grace**, i.e.- grace imparted by God in order to "minister" (or serve) other people; this is why **5** ministries are listed in Ephesians 4:11. By declaring that Mephibosheth was 5 at the time, the Lord is telling us that Mephibosheth represents, in a spiritual sense, those who have been imparted a grace to minister. Mephibosheth, spiritually speaking, was a **minister** in God's eyes, in the same way that all of His people are ministers under the New Covenant (Revelation 1:6, Isaiah 61:6, 1 Peter 2:9, 2 Corinthians 5:16-21).

Despite the fact that Mephibosheth represents a minister who had authority to walk on his own, his nurse decided to carry him in her arms when she decided to flee, in the same way that full-time ministers nowadays refuse to allow believers under their care to "walk" on their own (i.e.- to establish kingdom authority and to pronounce spiritual judgements, as we saw above). Since Mephibosheth's nurse was a "she", we can infer that God is referring here to the ministries in the Church that perform a "female" functionality; as we mentioned in a previous chapter[19], the ministries with a "female" functionality are "pastors" and "teachers". The Church is currently under a **pastoral matriarchy** that acts as an overprotective mother that smothers the spirit (i.e.- "male") authority of believers in the Body of Christ. Pastors create a state of constant **spiritual dependency** on them, doing the exact opposite of what good parents do. Even Joseph and Mary had a hard time accepting that Jesus was under their care for a **season**, and that, eventually, they would have to let Him go so that He could fulfil the Father's calling for His life (Luke 2:41-50, John 2:3-4, Matthew 12:46-50). Good parents want their children to learn to walk, to grow and become increasingly independent, until they are ready to make a life on their own. Bad parents manipulate their children into staying under their control, never letting go, even when the child has left home and is already married; they continue to meddle in the son's or daughter's life and matrimony, and are never willing to cut the

---

[19] pg. 52

umbilical cord. In such cases, however, not only the parent is at fault; God does indeed hold pastors accountable for creating a sense of constant dependency in believers, but God also holds believers accountable for **allowing** themselves to stay in such a spiritual dependency.

Notice how harsh Jesus's words were when Mary tried to maintain control over Him:

"*²And both Jesus was called, and his disciples, to the marriage. ³And when they wanted wine, the mother of Jesus saith unto him, They have no wine. ⁴Jesus saith unto her, **Woman, what have I to do with thee?** mine hour is not yet come.*" *(John 2:3-4)*

Jesus did not say, "Yes, mummy, whatever you say". By calling her, "woman", Jesus was saying to Mary, "Woman, your time is up; you were faithful as a mother in taking care of me, but now I have to **walk like a spirit**; Joseph and you were the father and mother of My **soul**, but don't forget that **God** is the Father of My spirit. Step aside, woman, and let God operate through Me."

As we saw in the chapter on "Canaanites", pastors are susceptible to being contaminated by Canaanite spirits. This is the reason why there is an interesting connexion in Scripture between the Canaanites and the Perizzites:

"*And there was a strife between the herdmen of Abram's cattle and the herdmen of Lot's cattle: and **the Canaanite and the Perizzite dwelled then in the land.**" *(Genesis 13:7)*

The word translated as "herdmen" in the passage above is the Hebrew word *raah*, which can also be translated as "shepherd" or "pastor". This means that the passage above speaks of a conflict between the pastors of Abram's cattle and the pastors of Lot's cattle. Abram means "*exalted father*", whilst Lot means "*covering*". "Abram-ic" pastors are those who act as good fathers who want those under their care to grow up **spiritually** and do greater things than they did themselves:

"*Verily, verily, I say unto you, He that believeth on me, the works that I do shall he do also; and **greater works than these shall he do**; because I go unto my Father.*" *(John 14:12)*

"Lot-ic" pastors, on the contrary, are those who want those under their care to remain under their "covering" forever. It is interesting to note that, after the conflict between Abram and Lot, it is Abram, not his nephew Lot, who decides that the best thing to do was for each to go their separate ways. Since Abram did not want to smother Lot under his covering, he was willing to let Lot go; this is what good parents do:

"*8And **Abram said unto Lot**, Let there be no strife, I pray thee, between me and thee, and between my herdmen and thy herdmen; for we be brethren. 9Is not the whole land before thee? **separate thyself, I pray thee, from me**: if thou wilt take the left hand, then I will go to the right; or if thou depart to the right hand, then I will go to the left." (Genesis 13:8-9)*

Canaanite pastors, i.e.- "Lot-ic" pastors, smother believers so much that they allow Perizzite spirits to enter the Church and cripple those believers. This is why the Holy Spirit took the time to mention the Canaanites and the Perizzites in Genesis 13:7. If you read the rest of Genesis chapter 13, you will notice that the Canaanites and the Perizzites are not mentioned again. We can therefore say that God mentions them in verse 7 in order to give us a spiritual clue as to what was going on **spiritually** when Abram and Lot separated.

To answer the question at the top of this section, we can say that Perizzite believers are crippled because of the spiritual over-protectiveness of Canaanite pastors and the so-called "ministers" in general.

Shame on you!

The meaning of Mephibosheth's name also reveals the participation of other spirits in the crippling of Perizzite believers. Mephibosheth means, "exterminating the shame", and comes from the Hebrew word *bosheth* meaning, "shame". The word *bosheth* comes from the word *buwsh* that means, "to put to shame, to be disappointed". As we studied in a previous chapter[20], the Jebusites are legalistic believers who love to humiliate others and put them to shame. To cause shame in another person is not wrong per se; sometimes it is the **right** thing to do, especially when we, as believers, speak words of judgement that are guided by the Spirit (1 Corinthians 6:5, 1 Corinthians 15:34, 2 Thessalonians 3:14, Titus 2:8). However, as we

---

[20] pg. 46

saw in the chapter on the "Jebusites"[21], Jebusites are enforcers of "spiritual castes", and they make a concerted effort to humiliate and put to shame believers whenever these believers begin to manifest their God-given spiritual authority.

One of the Jebusites' (and the Perizzites') favourite slogans is, "*Once small, always small*". If the first time they saw you, they saw you as a spiritual baby, they will **always** see you as a baby, no matter how much you grow in Christ. They will only be willing to listen to you when you are "publicly" recognised by some spiritual "authority" that they revere:

"*[54]And when he was come into his own country, he taught them in their synagogue, insomuch that they were astonished, and said, Whence hath this man this wisdom, and these mighty works? [55]Is not this the carpenter's son? is not his mother called Mary? and his brethren, James, and Joses, and Simon, and Judas? [56]And his sisters, are they not all with us? Whence then hath this man all these things? [57]And they were offended in him. But Jesus said unto them, A prophet is not without honour, save in his own country, and in his own house. [58]And he did not many mighty works there because of their unbelief.*" (Matthew 13:54-58)

"*[45]Then came the officers to the chief priests and Pharisees; and they said unto them, Why have ye not brought him? [46]The officers answered, Never man spake like this man. [47]Then answered them the Pharisees, Are ye also deceived? [48]Have any of the rulers or of the Pharisees believed on him? [49]But this people who knoweth not the law are cursed.*" (John 7:45-49)

Many Perizzite believers have bought into the idea that they are nothing but "small and insignificant believers" after years of being exposed to Jebusite believers who slap them in the face any time they claim to have a word from the Lord, especially when that word defies the orders or "teachings" of some Amorite superior authority. In a sense, the Jebusites are the "shamers", whilst the Perizzites are the "shamees". As we saw in the chapter on the "Jebusites", Jebusites provoke spiritual lameness in fellow believers. Because of their imposition of human judgements that promote human rules (as opposed to spiritual judgements that promote God's laws and will), Jebusites incapacitate believers and leave them begging next to the temple gate called "The Beautiful", i.e.- the door to grace (Acts

---

[21] pg. 33

3:2). Perizzites are beggars who do not realise that there is a wonderful door of access to God's grace available to them. They are starving spiritually without knowing that they have a great deal of spiritual currency deposited to their names in God's bank. Cursed be the Jebusites, and cursed be all those who cripple the spiritual authority of God's children!!!

*"¹At the same time came the disciples unto Jesus, saying, Who is the greatest in the kingdom of heaven? ²And Jesus called a little child unto him, and set him in the midst of them, ³And said, Verily I say unto you, Except ye be converted, and become as little children, ye shall not enter into the kingdom of heaven. ⁴Whosoever therefore shall humble himself as this little child, the same is greatest in the kingdom of heaven. ⁵And **whoso shall receive one such little child in my name receiveth me. ⁶But whoso shall offend one of these little ones which believe in me, it were better for him that a millstone were hanged about his neck, and that he were drowned in the depth of the sea.**" (Matthew 18:1-6)*

Just as the Jebusites love to slap small believers and shout "Shame on you!!" and "Shut up!!", God will slap the Jebusites in the face and shout,

> *Shame on you for putting My people to shame! Shame on you for stunting the growth of My little ones. Shut up, for it is **My** time to speak!!!*

God has prophesied that the Amorite-Jebusite-Canaanite stronghold on the Church will be broken:

*"¹⁰Also I brought you up from the land of Egypt, and led you forty years through the wilderness, to possess **the land of the Amorite**. ¹¹And I raised up of your sons for prophets, and of your young men for Nazarites. Is it not even thus, O ye children of Israel? saith the LORD. ¹²But **ye gave the Nazarites wine to drink**; and commanded the prophets, saying, Prophesy not. ¹³Behold, **I am pressed under you**, as a cart is pressed that is full of sheaves. ¹⁴Therefore the flight shall perish from the swift, and the strong shall not strengthen his force, neither shall the mighty deliver himself: ¹⁵Neither shall he stand that handleth the bow; and he that is swift of foot shall not deliver himself: neither shall he that rideth the horse deliver himself. ¹⁶And he that is courageous among the mighty shall flee away naked in that day, saith the LORD."* (Amos 2:10-16)

[The *Amorites* are referred to explicitly in verse 10. God's "little" believers are referred to in verse 11 when speaking of **sons** who are prophets and **young men** who are Nazarites. The *Canaanites* are referred to in verse 12 when speaking of those who give wine to the Nazarites. The *Jebusites* are also referred to in verse 12 when speaking of those who tell the prophets to shut up. The *Perizzite* oppression that tries to force believers to live as "villagers" with no spiritual hopes and dreams is referred to in verse 13.]

"I believe in angels"

Now that we have established the spiritual connexion between "cripples" and the Perizzite spirit, we can proceed to examine an attitude that is **very common** in Perizzite believers. This attitude can be observed in John chapter 5:

"¹After this there was a feast of the Jews; and Jesus went up to Jerusalem. ²Now there is at Jerusalem by the sheep market a pool, which is called in the Hebrew tongue Bethesda, having five porches. ³In these lay a great multitude of impotent folk, of blind, halt, withered, waiting for the moving of the water. ⁴For an angel went down at a certain season into the pool, and troubled the water: whosoever then first after the troubling of the water stepped in was made whole of whatsoever disease he had. ⁵And a certain man was there, which had an infirmity thirty and eight years. ⁶When Jesus saw him lie, and knew that he had been now a long time in that case, he saith unto him, Wilt thou be made whole? ⁷The impotent man answered him, Sir, I have no man, when the water is troubled, to put me into the pool: but while I am coming, another steppeth down before me. ⁸Jesus saith unto him, Rise, take up thy bed, and walk. ⁹And immediately the man was made whole, and took up his bed, and walked: and on the same day was the sabbath." (John 5:1-9)

The word "Bethesda" comes from the Hebrew words *beth*, meaning, "house", and *checed*, meaning, "mercy". Interestingly enough, the word *checed* can, at times, be also translated as "reproach, shame". "Bethesda", therefore, represents the modern-day Church, which has been converted from a **battle camp for spiritual soldiers** into a **mere "soul hospital" for weak, sickly, and crippled souls** who attend this "house of mercy" so that "expert doctors" (i.e.- pastors) may "tend to" their soul diseases; after all, "regular folks" are supposedly too spiritually "stupid" to do anything for themselves (or for each other) in God's Anointing. Any of these sickly patients who may dare to stand up and assert his or her spiritual authority is automatically put to shame. This is why Bethesda is not only the "house of mercy" but also the "house of shame". Bethesda, therefore, is a house where "mercy" is used as a subtle spiritual mechanism to preserve the separation between full-time "ministers" and "regular folks". Pastors are the spiritual doctors who went to "medical school" (i.e.- seminary) and are "intelligent enough" to treat the average believer's soul needs. As believers are taught that church is the place where they get "their needs met" (instead of the place where they are prepared for battle), believers are lulled into a crippling spiritual dependency on pastors. All battle camps have hospitals to treat the soldiers who are injured in battle, but the pastoral matriarchy, through its "gospel" of human mercy, has turned the Church into a Bethesda-type wasteland of dependent and crippled believers who can do nothing for themselves.

As you can see from the passage quoted above, a great multitude of crippled and blind people would wait by the pool of Bethesda, waiting for an "angel" to come and stir the waters. The word "angel" literally means "messenger", so it represents today's pastors. Today's believers are dependent on what the pastor does. If the pastor prays for them, they will be healed. If the pastor hears from God, they will have a word from the Lord. If the pastor blesses their activities, God's blessings are ensured. This is why the weak man from John chapter 5 above had been weak for **38 years**. This is the exact number of years that the people of Israel wandered aimlessly in the desert because of their disobedience:

"*14And the space in which we came from Kadeshbarnea, until we were come over the brook Zered, was **thirty and eight years; until all the generation of the men of war were wasted out from among the host**, as the LORD sware unto them. 15For indeed the hand of the LORD was against them, to destroy them from among the host, until they were consumed.*" (Deuteronomy 2:14-16)

The weak man of John chapter 5 waited 38 years for someone to take him to the waters when the angel stirred them (John 5:7). This man was dependent on the arm of flesh, not on God, and cursed is the man who trusts in the arm of flesh:

"*Thus saith the LORD; Cursed be the man that trusteth in man, and maketh flesh his arm, and whose heart departeth from the LORD.*" (Jeremiah 17:5)

From the two passages quoted above, we can infer that God's wrath is kindled against those who exercise a dependency on ministers and not on Him directly. Those who depend on man are made to wander in the desert until they die; this is why there are so many believers in church who may hold positions as deacons, teachers, elders, etc., whose callings have been cast away by God long, long ago. God cannot use people who relinquish their spiritual responsibility to grow. If you become a Perizzite believer, a "villager" with no spiritual visions and hopes (not only for yourself but for those around you), you are useless in His Kingdom. It is up to you, however, to reject the Perizzite doctrine. As crippled as your hands may be, the option to be free from a Perizzite influence is completely in your hands ... in the "hands" of your heart.

Who have you placed your faith in? Is your faith in "angels", i.e.- God's messengers, or have you placed your faith in God Himself. Most believers are "angel worshippers":

"[16]Let no man therefore judge you in meat, or in drink, or in respect of an holyday, or of the new moon, or of the sabbath days: [17]Which are a shadow of things to come; but the body is of Christ. [18]Let no man beguile you of your reward in a voluntary humility and worshipping of angels, intruding into those things which he hath not seen, vainly puffed up by his fleshly mind, [19]And not holding the Head, from which all the body by joints and bands having nourishment ministered, and knit together, increaseth with the increase of God. [20]Wherefore if ye be dead with Christ from the rudiments of the world, why, as though living in the world, are ye subject to ordinances, [21](Touch not; taste not; handle not; [22]Which all are to perish with the using;) after the commandments and doctrines of men? [23]Which things have indeed a shew of wisdom in will worship, and humility, and neglecting of the body; not in any honour to the satisfying of the flesh." (Colossians 2:16-23)

If you believe that being right with God consists of doing everything your local church authorities instruct you to do, you are an "angel worshipper", as verse 17 declares. Your walk with God does not consist of obeying external church rules and regulations. Your relationship with God is a **direct, face-to-face** relationship with Him in which you have direct experiences with Him and grow in Him, with your growth helping others to grow in Christ as well. Out of all the people who were lying at the pool of Bethesda, waiting for the waters to be stirred, the Lord Jesus went **directly** to the sick man. Through this, Jesus was trying to show this man that he had a direct line of communication with God. He did not have to depend on man to be healed. By going directly to him, Jesus was showing him that he was special to God, that God could distinguish him in a multitude. He was not just another ant in the anthill (I don't know about you, but, to me, all ants look alike). We are not insignificant "little" believers to God. Each one of us is special to Him, and He has mighty plans and purposes for each one of us:

"[13]Then were there brought unto him little children, that he should put his hands on them, and pray: and the disciples rebuked them. [14]But Jesus said, Suffer little children, and forbid them not, to come unto me: for of such is the kingdom of heaven. [15]And he laid his hands on them, and departed thence." (Matthew 19:13-15)

"Take heed that ye despise not one of these little ones; for I say unto you, That in heaven their angels do always behold the face of my Father which is in heaven." (Matthew 18:10)

When will we stop depending on man? It grieves and angers God's heart to see us behaving like Perizzite villagers.

So much more to say

There is so much more left to say about the Perizzite spirits!! Various passages in Scripture reveal that Perizzite spirits turn people into "simplistic judges", and other passages reveal that God's Spirit of Philadelphia[22] (the "undistorted" form of the Perizzite spirit), will be manifested during these latter days in God's prophetic remnant, bringing about the greatest revival mankind has ever seen. As the Perizzite spirit is defeated, the Spirit of Philadelphia is revealed.

---

[22] You may read more on the 7 Spirits of God, including the Spirit of Philadelphia, in a "Question & Answer" posting titled "What are the 7 sins and virtues?" posted on the Shamah-Elim website (http://shamah-elim.info/qa/q_7sinsvirt.htm).

To learn more about the Perizzite spirits, we recommend the following postings from the Shamah-Elim Bible Studies website:

- Prophetic word "Shame removed"
  (http://shamah-elim.info/p_shamermv.htm)
- Question & Answer "Trichotillomania"
  (http://shamah-elim.info/qa/q_trichtill.htm)
- Prophetic word "The broken EU net"
  (http://shamah-elim.info/p_brokeneu.htm)
- Question & Answer 'Is the Word "simple"?'
  (http://shamah-elim.info/qa/q_simple.htm)
- Prophetic word "Rain in Spain"
  (http://shamah-elim.info/p_spainrn.htm)
- Prophetic word "Floods in Eastern Europe"
  (http://shamah-elim.info/p_floodeu.htm)

Chapter 7
The Hivites

This chapter will focus on the "Hivites". The Hivite spirit is the spirit of self-indulgence and hedonistic self-centredness. It is the spirit that promotes the enjoyment of a false paradise on Earth; it tries to "prove" that God's nature is unnecessary in the equation of human life. Hivites believe that the pleasures they enjoy will certify the wisdom of the decision that Eve made in the Garden of Eden. Hivites are on a quest to prove that they can be like "gods" on this Earth without having to abide by God's ways.

An article similar to this chapter is posted on the Shamah-Elim Bible Studies website at the following web address:
http://shamah-elim.info/hivite.htm

What's in a name?
A great deal can be inferred directly from the meaning of the word "Hivite", which means, "villagers". If you already read the previous chapter, you will remember that "Perizzite" means "belonging to a village", which is very similar to the meaning of "Hivite". This implies that many of the things we said about the Perizzites also apply to Hivites. As we said with the Perizzites, villages have a connotation of "limited vision", implying that Hivites also have a **limited vision of life**. What makes them different from the Perizzites, however, is the **way** in which people under the influence of Hivite spirits limit their life.

The word "Hivite" is derived in Hebrew from the word *chavvah*, which means "life" or "living". In fact, *chavvah* is the Hebrew version of the name "Eve". This is why the Lord declares the following in Genesis:

*"And Adam called his wife's name **Eve**; because she was the mother of all **living**." (Genesis 3:20)*

Since the word "Hivite" is related to the concept of "**life**" in Hebrew, we can infer that the Hivites' vision of life is not one of limitation, poverty, and self-deprecation, as is the case with the Perizzites. On the contrary, **Hivites love to "live it up"**. Another interesting aspect can be derived from the **only** other appearance of the name "Eve" in the Old Testament:

116

*"And Adam knew Eve his wife; and she conceived, and bare Cain, and said, **I have gotten a man** from the LORD." (Genesis 4:1)*

The name "Cain" means, "possession"; this is why Eve said, "I have **gotten** a man from the Lord". The name "Cain", therefore, refers to possessing an inheritance handed down by someone else. From this, we can infer in the Spirit that Hivites are people who have **acquired some type of inheritance** that allows them the "freedom" to live "*la vida loca*". This is why the Hivite spirit is so prevalent in the sons and daughters of wealthy millionaires. Obviously, this does not mean that **all** descendants of millionaires are Hivites, but, it does mean that, if they are not careful, they can easily fall under the influence of Hivite spirits.

We must now ask ourselves the following: What does all of the above have to do with being a "villager"? The answer is simple if you observe Hivites carefully. Because of all the abundance and grace that surrounds them, they limit the vision of their lives to merely enjoying the wealth and fame built up by their parents (or even themselves). Hivites turn into people with few ambitions in life; all they want to do is to travel around the world and have a "good time". Some of you might be noticing that the Hivite spirit is, therefore, very common in people who have **retired**. Such people are prone to believing that they have nothing else to do in life but relax and enjoy the wealth they have accumulated during their earthly existence:

*"13And one of the company said unto him, Master, speak to my brother, that he divide the **inheritance** with me. 14And he said unto him, Man, who made me a judge or a divider over you? 15And he said unto them, Take heed, and beware of covetousness: for a man's life consisteth not in the abundance of the things which he possesseth. 16And he spake a parable unto them, saying, The ground of a certain rich man brought forth plentifully: 17And he thought within himself, saying, What shall I do, because I have no room where to bestow my fruits? 18And he said, This will I do: I will pull down my barns, and build greater; and there will I bestow all my fruits and my goods. 19And I will say to my soul, Soul, thou hast much goods laid up for many years; take thine ease, eat, drink, and be merry. 20But God said unto him, Thou fool, this night thy soul shall be required of thee: then whose shall those things be, which thou hast provided? 21So is he that layeth up treasure for himself, and is not rich toward God." (Luke 12:13-21)*

Notice how verses 13 and 14 above speak of possessing an "inheritance", which is related to what we said above about Cain and Eve, and is therefore related to the Hivite spirit. Notice also that the rich man in the parable above was **not** a lazy man, as certified by the following passage:

"[30]*I went by the field of the **slothful**, and by the vineyard of the man void of understanding;* [31]*And, lo, it was **all grown over with thorns**, and nettles had covered the face thereof, and the stone wall thereof was broken down.* [32]*Then I saw, and considered it well: I looked upon it, and received instruction.* [33]*Yet a little sleep, a little slumber, a little folding of the hands to sleep:* [34]*So shall thy poverty come as one that travelleth; and thy want as an armed man." (Proverbs 24:30-34)*

The rich man of Luke 12:16-21 was a hard-working man who took advantage of the fertile ground that he owned (v16). He was a Girgashite workaholic[23] motivated by "covetousness" or "greed", who longed to accumulate enough wealth so as to go into Hivite retirement where he could "eat, drink, and be merry" (Luke 12:19). Notice how the Lord Jesus ends the parable by declaring, in verse 21, that whosoever stores up treasure for **himself** is not rich in the eyes of God. This reveals another trait that is common to Hivites: they are **self-centred people** who only think about themselves. Hivites deceive themselves into thinking that the abundant grace that surrounds them is proof that the universe exists to serve them, instead of the other way around. A close study of Isaiah 38 and 39 reveals that king Hezekiah died a Hivite[24].

Three levels of grace

Hivite believers like to get drunk on the grace and blessings they are surrounded by, slowly forgetting that they are called to live a life of selfless sacrifice. Hivite believers turn God into their private waiter, a God who is there to satisfy every desire in their spoilt and bratty hearts:

"[1]*From whence come wars and fightings among you? come they not hence, even of your lusts that war in your members?* [2]*Ye lust, and have not: ye kill, and desire to have, and cannot*

---

[23] We share on "Girgashite workaholics" in pg. 22

[24] We share more on king Hezekiah's spiritual demise in an article titled "Are you a wide-gate believer?" posted on the Shamah-Elim website (http://shamah-elim.info/widegate.htm)

*obtain: ye fight and war, yet ye have not, because ye ask not. [3]Ye ask, and receive not, because ye ask amiss, that ye may consume it upon your lusts. [4]Ye adulterers and adulteresses, know ye not that the friendship of the world is enmity with God? whosoever therefore will be a friend of the world is the enemy of God. [5]Do ye think that the scripture saith in vain, The spirit that dwelleth in us lusteth to envy? [6]But **he giveth more grace**. Wherefore he saith, **God** resisteth the proud, but **giveth grace unto the humble**. [7]Submit yourselves therefore to God. Resist the devil, and he will flee from you. [8]Draw nigh to God, and he will draw nigh to you. Cleanse your hands, ye sinners; and purify your hearts, ye double minded. [9]Be afflicted, and mourn, and weep: let your laughter be turned to mourning, and your joy to heaviness. [10]Humble yourselves in the sight of the Lord, and he shall lift you up." (James 4:1-10)*

The word translated as "more" in verse 6 above is the Greek word *meizon*, which literally means, "greater". Verse 6 should then say, "But He gives greater grace", which means that those who seek after earthly things are given **a grace that imparts natural blessings**, but nothing more. A greater grace --- a grace of a higher level --- however, is given to those who humble themselves (v7), who submit to God's perfect will (v7), and who are willing to draw near to God (v8), even at the price of having to die to self in order to see His face (1 Timothy 6:16, Exodus 33:20, Genesis 32:26-31). Those who do these things receive **a grace and an authority to tear down spiritual strongholds and to manifest God's Glory and power on Earth** at a level that Hivite and Girgashite believers never will. In these last days, God will raise up a mighty Church full of consecrated believers who will take the spiritual atmosphere of the Earth by storm, and who will fill the Earth with God's presence and judgements like never before in human history (Psalm 105:1-7).

Hivites live biological lives of aimless wandering, as the Israelites did in the desert. The Israelites that provoked God's wrath and perished in the desert never lacked any material provision (Deuteronomy 29:4), but that did not mean that they were accepted by God:

"[1]Moreover, brethren, I would not that ye should be ignorant, how that all our fathers were under the cloud, and all passed through the sea; [2]And were all baptized unto Moses in the cloud and in the sea; [3]And did all eat the same spiritual meat; [4]And did all drink the same spiritual drink: for they drank of that spiritual Rock that followed them: and that Rock was Christ. [5]But with many of them God was not well pleased: for they were

*overthrown in the wilderness. [6]Now these things were our examples, to the intent we should not lust after evil things, as they also lusted. [7]Neither be ye **idolaters**, as were some of them; as it is written, The people sat down to eat and drink, and rose up to play." (1 Corinthians 10:1-7)*

*"[5]Mortify therefore your members which are upon the earth; fornication, uncleanness, inordinate affection, evil concupiscence, and covetousness, which is **idolatry**: [6]For which things' sake the wrath of God cometh on the children of disobedience" (Colossians 3:5-6)*

> [Notice how verse 5 of this passage links up with verse 7 of the previous passage through the word "idolatry"; notice also how the words "earth" and "covetousness" relate the passage above to Girgashite and Hivite spirits, as was seen when we looked at Luke 12:13-21 on pg. 117.]

The Israelites who perished in the desert received the grace that imparts natural blessings. On the contrary, the Israelites who crossed the Jordan with Joshua and conquered the Promised Land received a higher level of grace, a grace and authority to tear down spiritual strongholds and to manifest God's Glory and power on Earth. Which type of spiritual Israelite do you want to be? Which grace are you after?

Some might be wondering why this section is titled "**Three** levels of grace", considering that we have only mentioned **two** levels so far. The answer is that there is a level of grace that all human beings have access to, whether they believe in God or not (Matthew 5:45). Every human being is endowed with natural grace and abilities that the person has access to during his or her lifetime, even if he or she is never born again. To summarise, these are the three levels of grace:

Level of grace	Applies to...	Type	Provides...
Egyptian	All human beings, believers or unbelievers	Natural	Natural blessings and gifts
Desert	All believers, even those who are self-centred and who see God's grace as a means for self-satisfaction	Supernatural	Natural blessings and gifts that manifests God's mercy towards the person proper
Promised Land	Only believers who live selfless lives, and who are willing to go through suffering and death so that God's will may be fulfilled on Earth	Supranatural	Supernatural blessings and gifts that transcend into the spiritual atmosphere, tearing down spiritual kingdoms and manifesting God's glory and righteousness, thus transforming the lives of others

The soul trend of effeminate delight

The Old Testament ends with a very well-known prophetic word:

"*⁴Remember ye the law of Moses my servant, which I commanded unto him in Horeb for all Israel, with the **statutes and judgments**. ⁵Behold, **I will send you Elijah the prophet before the coming of the great and dreadful day of the LORD**: ⁶And he shall turn the heart of the fathers to the children, and the heart of the children to their fathers, lest I come and smite the earth with a curse." (Malachi 4:4-6)*

In Matthew 11, the Lord declares the following concerning the spirit of Elijah,

"*⁷And as they departed, Jesus began to say unto the multitudes concerning John, What went ye out into the wilderness to see? A reed shaken with the wind? ⁸But what went ye out for to see? **A man clothed in soft raiment? behold, they that wear soft clothing are in kings' houses**. ⁹But what went ye out for to see? A prophet? yea, I say unto you, and more than a prophet. ¹⁰For this is he, of whom it is written, Behold, I send my messenger before thy face, which shall prepare thy way before thee. ¹¹Verily I say unto you, Among them that are born of women there hath not risen a greater than John the Baptist: notwithstanding he that is least in the kingdom of heaven is greater than he. ¹²And from the days of John the Baptist until now the kingdom of heaven suffereth violence, and the violent take it by force. ¹³For all the prophets and the law prophesied until John. ¹⁴And if ye will receive it, this is Elias, which was for to come. ¹⁵He that hath ears to hear, let him hear." (Matthew 11:7-15)*

Just as the spirit of Elijah was sent to prepare the way for the manifestation of Christ in His **first** coming, the spirit of Elijah is here again to prepare the way for the manifestation of Christ in His **second** coming **through His remnant Church**. As Malachi 4:4 declares, this spirit will come with a "right-handed"[25] message of truth, justice, and judgement. Elijah will be heard by those who are willing to go out to uncomfortable wilderness (i.e.- the "lonely desert") to hear him (Matthew 11:7), which is a figure of those who are willing to be exposed to God's judgements outside the religious system (Deuteronomy 8:2).

---

[25] We share on spiritual "right-handedness" and "left-handedness" on pg. 64

Matthew 11:7 also declares that Elijah will not come as a "reed shaken by the wind". The word "reed" used here comes from the Greek word *kalamos*, which can also be translated as "staff" or "pen", referring, therefore, to the writing of God's laws. The word "wind" is translated from the Greek word *anemos*, from which the English word "animal" is derived. Since animals are souls without spirits, the word "wind" in Matthew 11:7 refers to trends and currents of thought and action driven by the soul, not the spirit. A "reed shaken by the wind", therefore, refers to people who "rewrite" God's laws to fit the "soul trends" and "fashions" of their day. In other words, they are people who adapt the "gospel" in order to make it pleasant to the hearer and not to God; they are the modern-day Aarons[26]. The spirit of Elijah, however, will come to defy these Aarons, who are driven by Canaanite "dancing" spirits.

Matthew 11:8 also declares that Elijah will not come as a man "clothed in soft raiment". The word "soft" used here comes from the Greek word *malakos*, which can also mean "effeminate" (and is translated as such in 1 Corinthians 6:9). As we said before[27], the spirit is usually represented in Scripture as a male figure, whilst the soul has a female connotation. **Men** clothed in "effeminate" raiment, therefore, refers to today's ministers who claim to be speaking in the spirit but who are really speaking from their souls, motivated by what other souls like to hear. As people who have used "soft" clothes will know, clothes made out of soft and delicate fabrics produce a sensation of pleasure and delight. This means that the phrase "clothed in soft raiment" also refers to people who are bent on seeking pleasure and comfort and whose main purpose is to enjoy the pleasures of this life. As we saw at the beginning of this chapter, this **hedonistic** approach to life is imparted by Hivite spirits.

Because of this desire for pleasure and satisfaction, Hivite believers become people who only go after the things that are soft, comfortable, and soothing. This "effeminate" tendency makes them **useless in the spiritual battlefield**. To be a good soldier, you must be willing to suffer, to endure hardship, to go through prolonged periods of material limitation and loneliness. God wants to raise a mighty army of soldiers filled with the Spirit of Elijah, believers who, like John the Baptist, are unafraid to live in the discomfort of the desert, eating locusts and wild honey instead of caviar and fillet mignon, and dressed in clothes made with camel hair (Matthew 3:1-

---

[26] We share more on the "modern-day Aarons" on pg. 84

[27] pg. 52

6). If you allow Hivite spirits to contaminate your soul, the Spirit of Elijah will not be on you, and you will not be part of the army that God wants to raise up in these last days; instead of fighting with that army, you will be judged by the army you shunned (Joel 2:1-11). Don't be a "softie"; fight the good fight:

"*³Thou therefore **endure hardness, as a good soldier of Jesus Christ.** ⁴No man that warreth entangleth himself with the affairs of this life; that he may please him who hath chosen him to be a soldier. ⁵And if a man also strive for masteries, yet is he not crowned, except he strive lawfully. ⁶The husbandman that laboureth must be first partaker of the fruits. ⁷Consider what I say; and the Lord give thee understanding in all things."* (2 Timothy 2:3-7)

The fact that we are called to be soldiers does not mean that all pleasure or blessings are wrong. As the passage above declares, those who labour in Him have the rights to be the "first partakers of the fruits". There is nothing more wonderful than living a life **in Christ**. It's a life full of purpose and meaning, but that meaning and purpose is derived from being willing to suffer and pay a price so that God's will and purposes may be established on Earth. Athletes who achieve greatness are those who are willing to make sacrifices. As the old saying goes, "No pain, no gain". Be willing to live for God and to obey Him, even if there will never be a temporal reward. Let your reward be **God Himself**, and I can assure you that God will also bless you with temporal rewards that will not only bless you in this life but will produce eternal blessings that will never pass away (these blessings are the "fruits" referred to in verse 6 above).

My friend, don't let yourself get run over by the soul trend of effeminate delight.

Today's Laodiceas

From Luke 12:21 (quoted on pg. 117), where the Lord says that Hivites are deceiving themselves into thinking that they are rich in the eyes of God, we can infer that the church of Laodicea in the book of Revelation was a church infested by Hivite spirits:

"*¹⁴And unto the angel of the church of the Laodiceans write; These things saith the Amen, the faithful and true witness, the beginning of the creation of God; ¹⁵I know thy works, that thou art neither cold nor hot: I would thou wert cold or hot. ¹⁶So then because thou art lukewarm, and neither cold nor hot, I will spue* *thee out of my mouth. [17]Because **thou sayest, I am rich**, and increased with goods, and have need of nothing; and **knowest not that thou art** wretched, and miserable, and **poor**, and blind, and naked: [18]**I counsel thee to buy of me gold tried in the fire, that thou mayest be rich**; and white raiment, that thou mayest be clothed, and that the shame of thy nakedness do not appear; and anoint thine eyes with eyesalve, that thou mayest see. [19]As many as I love, I rebuke and chasten: be zealous therefore, and repent." (Revelation 3:14-19)*

As we mentioned before[28], the Spirit of God that speaks to the church of Laodicea is the **Spirit of Prosperity**, as can be inferred from verse 18 above, where God's Spirit of Prosperity is telling Laodicea to buy gold tried in fire so that they may be **rich**. If one is spiritually sincere, one must admit that the word "rich" in verse 18 is referring to spiritual riches, since God first condemns Laodicea for thinking that they were "rich", when they were really poor. Please don't misunderstand me. I do not believe that material riches are wrong in and of themselves, and I do believe that God has **called** many people in the Body of Christ to be men and women with great material prosperity. To believe, however, that the level of your faith can be measured by how many digits your bank account balance has is a direct contradiction of Scripture, and, believe you me, if I have to choose between believing what a preacher says and what the Bible says, the Bible will win **every time**, no matter how famous, renowned, well-respected, or prosperous that preacher might be. Many preachers, including those who preach a great deal on prosperity, emphasise the first few passages of Hebrews chapter 11, the famous chapter on faith. They fail, however, to preach on the latter part of this chapter, since it goes against the grain of their preaching:

"[32]And what shall I more say? for the time would fail me to tell of Gedeon, and of Barak, and of Samson, and of Jephthae; of David also, and Samuel, and of the prophets: [33]Who through faith subdued kingdoms, wrought righteousness, obtained promises, stopped the mouths of lions, [34]Quenched the violence of fire, escaped the edge of the sword, out of weakness were made strong, waxed valiant in fight, turned to flight the armies of the aliens. [35]Women received their dead raised to life again: and others were tortured, not accepting deliverance; that they might obtain a better resurrection: [36]And others had trial of cruel mockings and scourgings, yea, moreover of bonds and

---

[28] pg. 87

imprisonment: *37They were stoned, they were sawn asunder, were tempted, were slain with the sword: they wandered about in sheepskins and goatskins; **being destitute**, afflicted, tormented; 38(Of whom the world was not worthy:) they wandered in deserts, and in mountains, and in dens and caves of the earth. 39And these all, having obtained a good report through faith, received not the promise: 40God having provided some better thing for us, that they without us should not be made perfect." (Hebrews 11:32-40)*

Notice how this passage speaks of **faithful** believers who suffered, were slain, and wandered about in **destitution** and affliction (verse 37). Doesn't this prove that God did not command us "to walk by faith" in order to have earthly contentment and wealth? Doesn't this prove that you can be in God's perfect will and still suffer? Some hard-hearted (but intelligent) prosperity preachers might be saying to themselves, *"the **poor** writer of this book hasn't noticed verse 40, where God says that He has something better for us than what those **poor** men suffered"*, insinuating, therefore, that faith and suffering were intertwined in the Old Testament only.

I would encourage such preachers to read chapter 12 of Hebrews (which follows directly after the passage quoted above), where God calls us to run the race with patience and to be encouraged by the sufferings of the Anointed One (Christ) so that we may not faint when we suffer ourselves. Chapter 12 of Hebrews then proceeds to speak of a God who causes suffering in order to discipline us to and spur our growth in Him. Chapter 12 then speaks of not allowing ourselves to become bitter because of God's disciplines (i.e.- His judgements), lest we become like Edom, who forsook his spiritual inheritance for a temporary satisfaction:

"15Looking diligently lest any man fail of the grace of God; lest any root of bitterness springing up trouble you, and thereby many be defiled; 16Lest there be any fornicator, or profane person, as Esau, who for one morsel of meat sold his birthright. 17For ye know how that afterward, when he would have inherited the blessing, he was rejected: for he found no place of repentance, though he sought it carefully with tears." (Hebrews 12:15-17)

Despite all of the evidence above, someone out there might still be saying, *"Look, the birthright and the 'blessing' in the passage above refers to **material** prosperity"*, to which I would soundly reply, "No way, Jose". Why? Because, Jacob never felt like he had the "blessing" until that fateful night when he struggled with the angel of God until the break of dawn:

"*24And Jacob was left alone; and there wrestled a man with him until the breaking of the day. 25And when he saw that he prevailed not against him, he touched the hollow of his thigh; and the hollow of Jacob's thigh was out of joint, as he wrestled with him. 26And he said, Let me go, for the day breaketh. And he said, **I will not let thee go, except thou bless me**. 27And he said unto him, What is thy name? And he said, Jacob. 28And he said, Thy name shall be called no more Jacob, but Israel: for as a prince hast thou power with God and with men, and hast prevailed. 29And Jacob asked him, and said, Tell me, I pray thee, thy name. And he said, Wherefore is it that thou dost ask after my name? And he blessed him there. 30And Jacob called the name of the place Peniel: for I have seen God face to face, and my life is preserved. 31And as he passed over Penuel the sun rose upon him, and **he halted upon his thigh**. 32Therefore the children of Israel eat not of the sinew which shrank, which is upon the hollow of the thigh, unto this day: because he touched the hollow of Jacob's thigh in the sinew that shrank." (Genesis 32:24-32)*

If you read the beginning of Genesis chapter 32, you will notice that, at the time of this struggle with the angel of the Lord, Jacob **already was** a very wealthy man, but he knew that the "blessing" he was after was still not his. Otherwise, why would he ask God to "bless" him in verse 26? Notice also that the "blessing" came together with an **impairment**. Even though Jacob was spiritually blessed that dawn, he came out of the blessing **limping**, as a sign of the spiritual judgement that God had executed on him for being a man so resourceful and self-reliant all of his life (this is why, when speaking of God's chastising judgements, Hebrews 12 mentions "lame" or "limping" feet in verse 13).

For those who might still be convinced that there is something wrong with a person's faith if he or she is not rich, consider the following verses:

"*9I know thy works, and tribulation, and **poverty, (but thou art rich)** and I know the blasphemy of them which say they are Jews, and are not, but are the synagogue of satan." (Revelation 2:9)*

"[12]*I know both how to be abased*, and I know *how to abound*: every where and in all things I am instructed both to be full and to be hungry, *both to abound and to suffer need*. [13]*I can do all things through Christ which strengtheneth me.* [14]*Notwithstanding ye have well done, that ye did communicate with my affliction.*" (Philippians 4:12-14)

"[9]*For I think that God hath set forth us the apostles last, as it were appointed to death: for we are made a spectacle unto the world, and to angels, and to men.* [10]*We are fools for Christ's sake, but ye are wise in Christ; we are weak, but ye are strong; ye are honourable, but we are despised.* [11]**Even unto this present hour we both hunger, and thirst, and are naked, and are buffeted, and have no certain dwellingplace**; [12]*And labour, working with our own hands: being reviled*, we bless; being persecuted, we suffer it: [13]Being defamed, we intreat: we are made as the filth of the world, and are the offscouring of all things unto this day.*" (1 Corinthians 4:9-13)

Does all of the above sound like faith and suffering are only intertwined in the Old Testament? Does it sound as if God is calling us to live a pleasant life of spiritual Hivite retirement, where all we have to do is receive His material blessings and wait until we are taken in the rapture? If it were so, those of us who long to live a life of obedience and faith (and who have been willing to pay a high price so that God's will may be fulfilled in our lives and in the lives of others) are **big-time fools**:

"[30]*And **why stand we in jeopardy every hour**? [31]I protest by your rejoicing which I have in Christ Jesus our Lord, **I die daily**. [32]If after the manner of men I have fought with beasts at Ephesus, **what advantageth it me, if the dead rise not**? let us eat and drink; for to morrow we die. [33]Be not deceived: evil communications corrupt good manners. [34]Awake to righteousness, and sin not; for some have not the knowledge of God: I speak this to your shame.*" (1 Corinthians 15:30-34)

Today's Laodiceas, therefore, are the congregations where grace and prosperity are emphasised so much that the word of truth, righteousness, and judgement is ignored. As we said before[29], a "gospel" of grace without truth, a left-handed "gospel", draws in Hittite spirits that drive people to live biological lives **without a sense of prophetic purpose**, without a willingness to pay a spiritual price so

---

[29] pg. 68

that God's Glory may be manifested in others. I believe that it brings tears to God's eyes, as it does mine, to see so many brothers and sisters, with such great and mighty callings and gifts, throwing their spiritual inheritance away for the sake of a life of natural contentment, aimlessly wandering as the Israelites did in the desert.

As a "gospel" that emphasises material prosperity is preached in a congregation, Hittite and Hivite spirits are drawn in, eventually turning the congregation into a spiritual Laodicea "deserving" of the harsh words that God pronounces against that church in Revelation 3:14-19. There are modern-day Laodiceas all over the world. However, there is a region of the world that has become the most deserving of the title "**Modern-day Laodicea**", and that region is Latin America...

A word on Latin America

God has blessed Latin America greatly in the spiritual, political, and economic realms, and the percentage of Christian believers has increased dramatically in the last few decades. Unfortunately, Latin America (L.A.) is now infested with pastors who preach a Hivite and Hittite message that emphasises grace and blessings alone. The Latin American revival is a sad example of how believers can forget the Righteous Giver and focus on the pleasant gifts. In Latin America, pastors preach a message that says,

"If you become a Christian, you will be prosperous, your family will be happy, and you will not suffer nor be sick; and, if you are sick, we, the mighty and glorious ministers, have been sent by God to relieve you of your suffering"

This is done in order to draw as many people to the "gospel" as possible. Latin American pastors are consumed with the goal of building larger temples and having larger congregations, instead of being consumed by the desire to see the manifestation of God's Glory through His people. Latin American pastors want to see miracles (and they are seeing them); they want to "feel" a spiritual presence (and they are feeling it), but they want all of this whilst staying in control, without allowing the "little" believers to manifest all the potential that is inside of them. L.A. pastors are trying to bring the Ark of the Covenant on a new cart (2 Samuel 6:3), using all the new evangelism tools and techniques that are in vogue, refusing to bring the Ark on the spiritual shoulders of nameless priests (1 Chronicles 15:1, 15:15; Joel 2:12-17) because that would mean that **man** (i.e.- the pastors) would no longer be in control of what can happen. They want God's glory to come, as long as they can shine along with that glory. They have shut up the prophets, and refuse to hear the voice of God, Whose desire is to raise up **a mighty people** instead of just **mighty pastors**:

*"⁹Then said he unto me, Prophesy unto the wind, prophesy, son of man, and say to the wind, Thus saith the Lord GOD; Come from the four winds, O breath, and breathe upon these slain, that they may live. ¹⁰So I prophesied as he commanded me, and the breath came into them, and they lived, and stood up upon their feet, **an exceeding great army**. ¹¹Then he said unto me, Son of man, these bones are the whole house of Israel: behold, they say, Our bones are dried, and our hope is lost: we are cut off for our parts. ¹²Therefore prophesy and say unto them, Thus saith the Lord GOD; Behold, O my people, I will open your graves, and cause you to come up out of your graves, and bring you into the land of Israel. ¹³And ye shall know that I am the LORD, when I have opened your graves, O my people, and brought you up out of your graves, ¹⁴And shall put my spirit in you, and ye shall live, and I shall place you in your own land: then shall ye know that I the LORD have spoken it, and performed it, saith the LORD." (Ezekiel 37:9-14)*

*"²⁵But Jesus called them unto him, and said, **Ye know that the princes of the Gentiles exercise dominion over them**, and **they that are great exercise authority upon them**. ²⁶But **it shall not be so among you**: but whosoever will be great among you, let him be your minister; ²⁷And whosoever will be chief among you, let him be your servant: ²⁸Even as the Son of man came not to be ministered unto, but to minister, and to give his life a ransom for many." (Matthew 20:25-28)*

Not only have the pastors strayed from God's purpose in Latin America; believers there, in general, are comfortable with the Hivite-oriented "gospel" they are hearing. They rejoice over the idea of delegating the responsibility of "spiritual growth" to their ministers because it frees them up to follow their Girgashite and Hivite pursuits. In churches all over Latin America, Jebusites are slapping[30] the few **true** prophets in the face, coercing them into a submission to man that denies what God has spoken to their hearts:

"⁴¹Then Peter said unto him, Lord, speakest thou this parable unto us, or even to all? ⁴²And the Lord said, Who then is that faithful and wise steward, whom his lord shall make ruler over

---

[30] We share more on how Jebusites "slap" others on pg. 44

*his household, to give them their portion of meat in due season? ⁴³Blessed is that servant, whom his lord when he cometh shall find so doing. ⁴⁴Of a truth I say unto you, that he will make him ruler over all that he hath. ⁴⁵But and if that servant say in his heart, My lord delayeth his coming; and shall begin **to beat the menservants and maidens, and to eat and drink, and to be drunken;** ⁴⁶The lord of that servant will come in a day when he looketh not for him, and at an hour when he is not aware, and will cut him in sunder, and will appoint him his portion with the unbelievers. ⁴⁷And that servant, which knew his lord's will, and prepared not himself, neither did according to his will, shall be beaten with many stripes. ⁴⁸But he that knew not, and did commit things worthy of stripes, shall be beaten with few stripes. For unto whomsoever much is given, of him shall be much required: and to whom men have committed much, of him they will ask the more. ⁴⁹I am come to send fire on the earth; and what will I, if it be already kindled?" (Luke 12:41-49)*

God gave a spiritual mantle to Latin America, a calling to be the ground base from which God would launch a latter-day revival that would shake the world. On 29 June, 2003, however, this spiritual mantle was stripped from Latin America, in the same way that the kingdom of Israel was stripped from Saul (1 Samuel 15:27-28). This mantle has now been given back to the United States and Europe, despite all of their faults (Matthew 21:43, 22:1-10). Over the next 10 years, you will see how the evangelical movement in Latin America will enter a state of spiritual stagnation and decadence, until it will become evident to all the world that something had been inherently wrong for many years with the "revival" in Latin America. The modern-day Laodicea has been vomited out of God's mouth (Revelation 3:16) because it preferred to get drunk on Hivite grace and rejected God's prophetic purpose, which called for a price that they were unwilling to pay in their hearts. They preferred the "gospel" that preaches about the "balm of Gilead" that soothes and comforts, and decided to forget about the "sword of justice and judgement" that brings true healing and restoration (Isaiah 1:27, Isaiah 33:22-24). The Lord has therefore sent Hittite spirits of deceit to ensure that Latin America and all other modern-day Laodiceas get drunk on left-handed grace; these spirits of deceit are designed to make them feel convinced that God is "with them", but they will suddenly realise that things were not as "hunky dory" as they thought:

*"²⁷Therefore thou shalt say unto them, Thus saith the LORD of hosts, the God of Israel; **Drink ye, and be drunken, and spue,***

and fall, and rise no more, because of the sword which I will send among you. ^{28}*And it shall be, if they refuse to take the cup at thine hand to drink, then shalt thou say unto them, Thus saith the LORD of hosts; Ye shall certainly drink.* ^{29}*For, lo, I begin to bring evil on the city which is called by my name, and should ye be utterly unpunished? Ye shall not be unpunished: for I will call for a sword upon all the inhabitants of the earth, saith the LORD of hosts." (Jeremiah 25:27-29)*

"^{10}For this is the day of the Lord GOD of hosts, a day of vengeance, that he may avenge him of his adversaries: and the sword shall devour, and it shall be satiate and made drunk with their blood: for the Lord GOD of hosts hath a sacrifice in the north country by the river Euphrates. ^{11}**Go up into Gilead, and take balm, O virgin,** *the daughter of Egypt:* **in vain shalt thou use many medicines; for thou shalt not be cured."** *(Jeremiah 46:10-11)*

As many of you may know, Ezekiel chapter 47 speaks of the River of God, which is a figure of the Church's latter-day revival. In the middle of this worldwide revival, however, there will be "miry places", places of spiritual stagnation; Latin America will be one of them. At the time of this writing (July 10, 2004), only 3 nations in that region **still** have an opportunity of manifesting God's Glory in the latter days: Argentina, Brazil, and Uruguay. But, if they are not careful, they will also be part of that spiritual place called the "**Latin American swamp**":

"^{10}And it shall come to pass, that the fishers shall stand upon it from Engedi even unto Eneglaim; they shall be a place to spread forth nets; their fish shall be according to their kinds, as the fish of the great sea, exceeding many. ^{11}But **the miry places thereof** *and the* **marishes thereof shall not be healed***; they shall* **be given to salt."** *(Ezekiel 47:10-11)*

Latin America will be left like Lot's wife (Genesis 19:26), as a pillar of salt that will serve as a spiritual example (2 Peter 2:5-6) of God's judgement over a region that received so much from God but which perverted and misused all the wonderful blessings that God had given it:

"^{4}For **it is impossible for those who were once enlightened,** *and have tasted of the heavenly gift, and were made partakers of the Holy Ghost,* ^{5}*And have tasted the good word of God, and the powers of the world to come,* ^{6}*If they shall fall away,* **to**

renew them again unto repentance; seeing they crucify to themselves the Son of God afresh, and put him to an open shame. ^{7}*For the earth which drinketh in the rain that cometh oft upon it, and bringeth forth herbs meet for them by whom it is dressed, receiveth blessing from God:* ^{8}*But **that which beareth thorns and briers is rejected, and is nigh unto cursing; whose end is to be burned.***" (Hebrews 6:4-8)

All of the above is not only God's Word against Latin America but also God's Word against **all** places and peoples where Hivite spirits are allowed to pervert His Gospel.

The "La" in Laodicea stands for "Latin america".

So much more to say

There is so much more left to say about the Hivite spirits!! Much can be discerned regarding the Hivite spirit by studying Genesis 34, which speaks of Shechem, the son of Hamor the Hivite. Much can also be discerned by studying the Gibeonite **covenant** mentioned in Joshua 9 (the Gibeonites were Hivites, according to Joshua 9:7). These passages show how the Hivites love to make covenants birthed out of **convenience of the soul**, as opposed to **conviction of the spirit**. These passages also reinforce many of the spiritual principles already stated in this chapter.

To learn more about the Hivite spirits, we recommend the following postings from the Shamah-Elim Bible Studies website:

  * Article "Easy like Sunday morning"
    (http://shamah-elim.info/easy.htm)
  * Prophetic word "Hurricane Frances"
    (http://shamah-elim.info/p_hurrfran.htm)
  * Prophetic word "Floods in Eastern Europe"
    (http://shamah-elim.info/p_floodeu.htm)
  * Prophetic word "Katrina is hard on Big Easy (Part 2)"
    (http://shamah-elim.info/p_katrina2.htm)

Chapter 8
The triangle of evil

Now that we have studied each of the 7 evil spirits that we must fight against, we must briefly consider how they are related to each other. This chapter will focus on these spirits' general inter-connexion by considering three different parameters.

Part of this chapter's content is similar to part of an article posted on the Shamah-Elim Bible Studies website at the following web address:
http://shamah-elim.info/rvvlblvr.htm

Right vs. left

One parameter to consider is whether each spirit is **"right-handed"** or **"left-handed"**. As we studied earlier[31], the right side is a side of "limitation" and "scarcity", whilst the left side is a side of "freedom" and "excesses". Therefore, we can say that the **Jebusite** spirit is right-handed because it is a spirit of humanistic legalism that limits others by "slapping" them into submission to man-made laws. The **Girgashite** spirit is also right-handed because it limits man to the natural realm, scoffing at anything that sounds too "spiritual". A close study of the Girgashite spirit[32] also reveals that it turns people into strict followers of methods and procedures; to Girgashites, the "method" is more important than the persons the method was made for. Girgashites tend to box other people within purposeless paradigms, and they frown upon anyone who may dare to fly above the earthly methodologies they unquestioningly bind themselves to. Therefore, it is safe to say that Girgashites are right-handed.

As we clearly saw when we studied the **Hittite** spirit, Hittites are left-handed because they are spirits of chaos that target the emotions, meaning that they promote "freedom" unbridled by the truth. The **Canaanite** spirit is also left-handed because Canaanites target the emotions to promote the pursuit of lowly passions. Canaanites work to shut down the mind, in an effort to prevent it making judgements; as they disable judgement-making, Canaanites emotionally

---

[31] pg. 61

[32] We share more on the connexion between the Girgashite spirit and human methodologies in an article titled "The stingy enemies of God" posted on the Shamah-Elim website (http://shamah-elim.info/stgenemy.htm)

pressure people into pleasing others rather than pleasing God, which leads to carnal excesses that transgress the truth.

The **Hivite** spirit is also left-handed because it is a spirit of excess that promotes self-indulgence in inherited grace. By contrast, the **Perizzite** spirit is right-handed because it confines people to a life of hopeless smallness and low self-esteem.

Of the 7 evil spirits, the only spirit that cannot be labelled as purely "right-handed" or "left-handed" is the **Amorite** spirit, since it manifests both. Amorites are earthly kings who at times impose right-handed law through their Jebusite officers, and at times impose left-handed terror and fear in their subjects through covert intimidation.

The above can be summarised as follows:

Evil spirit	Left	Right
Girgashites		X
Jebusites		X
Amorites	---	---
Hittites	x	
Canaanites	x	
Perizzites		X
Hivites	x	

Villager?

A second parameter to consider is whether the spirit is a "village" spirit. As you may remember, the only spirits whose names mean "villagers" are the **Perizzites** and the **Hivites**. The Perizzites are "village spirits" that cause people to resign themselves to a limited life of "spiritual poverty" because they are "too small and insignificant" to dream. The Hivites, on the other hand, are "village spirits" that cause people to limit their vision of life to a hedonistic enjoyment of riches. Village spirits breed isolation from reality. Whilst the Perizzite spirit breeds isolation from the world of possibilities, the Hivite spirit breeds isolation from the world of responsibilities.

"Village" spirits enclose people by blinding their vision. Once a village spirit takes hold of a person, darkness quickly ensues.

Earth-related?

A third parameter to consider is whether the spirit's name has the connotation of "earth" to it. Of the 7 evil spirits, the only two whose names are earth-related are the "**Canaanites**" (which means, "low*lands*") and the "**Girgashites**" (which means, "*clay* dwellers").

Earth-related spirits reduce people to the "animal" level. People dominated by these spirits become very passive when it comes to things that go beyond the natural realm. To such people, whatever is not visible to the natural mind or able to be felt by natural emotions becomes irrelevant. In a sense, they become "dead" to such things, and they turn into mere biological beings who live by natural understanding and natural instincts. The earth-related spirits drain all the extraordinary qualities of those under their influence, turning them into "common" and "ordinary", as common and ordinary as the dust of the Earth.

Putting it all together

We can now combine the 3 parameters into the following table:

Evil spirit	Right vs. Left	Village spirit?	Earth-related?
Girgashites	Right-handed	No	Yes
Jebusites	Right-handed	No	No
Amorites	(Neither)	No	No
Hittites	Left-handed	No	No
Canaanites	Left-handed	No	Yes
Perizzites	Right-handed	Yes	No
Hivites	Left-handed	Yes	No

The above table allows us to place these 7 spirits in such a way that the following triangle is formed:

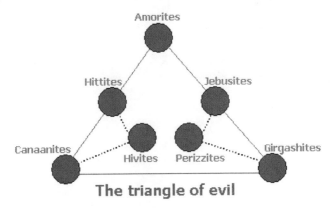

The triangle of evil

The motivation for the placement shown above is the following:

- The Amorites appear in the middle, because they are neither right-handed nor left-handed.

- The Amorites appear at the top of the triangle because they are spirits of "earthly kingship"; the Amorites are the pinnacle, the "strong men" of the hierarchy of evil.

- The Jebusites, Girgashites, and Perizzites appear on the right side because they are "right-handed" spirits.

- The Hittites, Canaanites, and Hivites are placed on the left side because they are "left-handed" spirits.

- The Perizzites and Hivites are placed **inside** the triangle because they are "village spirits" that enclose people by blinding their vision.

- The Jebusites and Hittites are placed immediately below the Amorites because they act as the "authorities" that enforce the Amorite's kingdom. The Jebusites are the Amorite's police force, and the Hittites are the Amorite's "secret service". Even though Hittites may seem as "independent loose cannons", they are, at the end, undercover forces that fight in favour of an Amorite spirit's interests.

- The Girgashites and Canaanites are placed at the base of the triangle because they are "earth-related", meaning that they act as the "ground base" that sustains the hierarchy of evil spirits on Earth.

This triangle has worked to trap and enslave mankind, but God has sent His righteous remnant into the Earth to break this cursed triangle. You become a member of this remnant through the choices in your heart. If your heart is after the Spirit nature of God and not after the soul nature of fallen man, you shall be a triangle breaker.

Made in the USA
Lexington, KY
16 February 2012